Praise for Wendy

121 First

"Ever feel like you're royally screwed when it comes to dating? Like you're more likely to be kidnapped by terrorists than find Mr. Right? This is your book. Wendy is like your awesomest girlfriend, only she actually gives good dating advice. She'll make you laugh with her whip smart remarks, cheer you up, cheer you on, and encourage you every step of the way."

—**Linda Sivertsen**, bestselling author and creator of
The Boyfriend Log iPhone dating app

"With a warm, experienced, 'been-there, done-that' tone, Wendy Newman not only chronicles the many challenges for women navigating the modern dating world, but she also reframes them in such a manner that will make even the most jaded dater breathe a sigh of relief. While most self-help books tell you what you want to hear, Newman tells you what you need to hear with such compassion that you'll probably want to email her in six months to tell her that you listened to her advice and finally found love."

—**Evan Marc Katz**, dating coach and author

"Wendy Newman takes the mystery, the game playing, and strategizing out of dating. She went on 121 first dates, so you can short-cut your journey into the partnership that's in your future. Brilliant. A masterpiece. The best dating book I've read in a decade."

—**Julie Ferman**, personal matchmaker and dating coach,
www.JulieFerman.com

"If you feel uncomfortable about dating or you're dreading jumping into dating online, *121 First Dates* is for you! No formulaic tips, tricks, or rules to follow, Wendy's is an authentic and realistic approach that will have you feeling more confident about dating, no matter your age, body type, or personal struggles. She'll give you the sense that being yourself is better than okay. *121 First Dates* is more than a dating guide—it's a manual for empowered living!"

—**"Bombshell Betty" Betty Field**, pinup, burlesque,
and body image maven

Praise for Wendy Newman's

121
Dates

"When I first read *121 First Dates*, it was like 'Wow, so that's where I went wrong…and bam! That's how I can fix it!' Wendy nailed it!"
—**Esha Mohanh**, *Behind the Look LA*

"*121 First Dates* is a refreshing, riveting, insightful, and eye-opening look into relationships, romance, courting, and sexuality. Wendy Newman's work offers a profound punch that immediately wakes you up to the glory and magic of romance while journeying through the eyes of passion, sensuality, and true partnership and oneness. If you are looking to unravel the mystery of love then this book is for you."
—**Nicole Brandon**, motivational speaker, life coach, author, actress, and the CEO of Artistry In Motion (A.I.M. For Excellence Inc.)

"Wendy helps would-be daters get their feet wet in the seemingly murky pond of online dating and meeting men in the real world. She shares mortifying and hilarious moments as well as useful tips on flirting, self-care, and how to be your best self while finding the best guy for you. Do yourself a favor and read this book."
—**Marie Benard**, talk show host at CiTR 101.9 FM Vancouver, B.C.

"The first date you should make is with *121 First Dates*, sit down with a glass of wine and dive right in. You'll learn more about dating than you even thought to ask."
—**Grae Drake**, film commentator and TV host, *Rotten Tomatoes*

"Sadly, the normal process of dating usually robs women of our most attractive, fall-in-love-with qualities: self-confidence, authenticity, and passion. Wendy Newman is out to change all that with delightful wit, compassion, and humor. The judgment-free zone located within the pages of *121 First Dates* playfully guides women through the dating process, while granting them the freedom and permission to find what they truly need in a relationship."
—**Alison A. Armstrong**, author of *The Queen's Code*

"Wendy Newman has created a smart, engaging, and compassionate dating guide for women. She shares her victories, struggles, and mistakes without apology in the hopes that her journey will inspire others to live to their full love potential."
—**Sheila Kelley**, creator of Sheila Kelley S Factor and author of *The S Factor*

121 First Dates

How to Succeed at Online Dating, Fall in Love, and Live Happily Ever After (Really!)

Wendy Newman

ATRIA PAPERBACK
New York London Toronto Sydney New Delhi

BEYOND WORDS
Hillsboro, Oregon

ATRIA PAPERBACK
An Imprint of Simon & Schuster, Inc.
1230 Avenue of the Americas
New York, NY 10020

BEYOND WORDS
20827 N.W. Cornell Road, Suite 500
Hillsboro, Oregon 97124-9808
503-531-8700 / 503-531-8773 fax
www.beyondword.com

Managing editor: Lindsay S. Brown
Editor: Emily Han, Sylvia Spratt
Copyeditor: Linda M. Meyer
Proofreader: Jade Chan
Cover design: Devon Smith
Composition: William H. Brunson Typography Services

First Atria Paperback/Beyond Words trade paperback edition January 2016

For more information about special discounts for bulk purchases, please contact
Simon & Schuster Special Sales at 1-866-506-1949 or business@simonandschuster.com.

The Simon & Schuster Speakers Bureau can bring authors to your live event. For more
information or to book an event, contact the Simon & Schuster Speakers Bureau at
1-866-248-3049 or visit our website at www.simonspeakers.com.

Manufactured in the United States of America

10 9 8 7 6 5 4 3 2 1

Library of Congress Cataloging-in-Publication Data

Newman, Wendy,
    121 first dates : how to succeed at online dating, fall in love, and live happily ever after
(really!) / Wendy Newman.
        pages cm
    1. Dating (Social customs).   2 Online dating.   3. Man-woman relationships.
4. Mate selection.   I. Title.   II. Title: One hundred twenty one first dates.
HQ801.N486   2016
306.73—dc23

2015023228

ISBN 978-1-58270-572-9
ISBN 978-1-5011-1147-1 (eBook)

The corporate mission of Beyond Words Publishing, Inc.: *Inspire to Integrity*

For my mother, Susan Bailess.
Thank you for teaching me to be fearless.

Contents

Part II: The First Date

Part III: After the First Date

An expert is a person who has made all the mistakes
that can be made in a very narrow field.

—Niels Bohr
Nobel Prize–winning physicist

Introduction:
A Day in the Life of a Dater

5:52 PM: It's pick-an-outfit time. Thankfully, it only takes six tries before I land the magical combination. I examine my reflection and critique every detail. *Almost there . . . look again*, I half scold myself as if I were talking to my little sister. I hate these shoes, only two inches high. Shawn says he's six feet tall. That's guy code for five-foot-ten. I've learned that one the hard way.

Black Lycra leggings cover my two finest features: long, pasty-white but perpetually toned legs. The leggings serve a dual purpose: they hold me together and combat the chilly San Francisco fog. No jewelry on my fingers; a silver oversized heart around my neck as a subliminal message of availability; and the main event: the perfect black dress. Not the cocktail-attire "little black dress" you see in magazines. Fashion magazines aren't designed for women like me. Stores aren't well equipped to handle me, either.

When it comes to clothing, I live in a neighborhood called "no man's land." An XL is often too tight, but I'm too small for anything plus-size. I live squarely in that gap. The preferred curvy girl's shape is the hourglass. Yeah, that's not me, either. I'm more of an apple—not even lucky enough to carry any junk in my trunk. I'm not complaining, mind you, but merely drawing a picture of myself because I want you to know that I'm neither young nor thin. And yet dating happens for me despite all those cultural "prerequisites" I'm supposedly lacking. So how does it happen? I'm determined and I leverage what I've got—meaning that I highlight what works. Because, this body is where I live.

Preparation for this evening started hours ago at a posh salon: manicure, pedicure (not that Shawn will be allowed to see that), waxing of the upper lip and chin, and reshaping my brows. (The talent for brow shaping has to be top-notch; I'm in my mid-forties, so the aesthetician's got to be able to pluck out all the white ones without leaving big bald patches. It's tricky.)

Next stop, the hair stylist, where my long red-brown hair is professionally shampooed, blow-dried, and styled for twenty-two dollars. The two stops total a hundred and thirty bucks, all so I can be "salon ready" while sporting an attitude that says, "Yes, I always look like this."

Shawn and I met on OkCupid, an online dating site. We'd written to each other nearly every day over two and half weeks. At first, I wasn't that excited. I was in one of those moods. You know the one: I resented being single. I was weary of online dating, but after giving in to the pressure of friends telling me it was time to get back to it, I resigned myself to resuming the search. The website indicated that Shawn and I were a 94 percent match—94 percent. Why not? I contacted him first, and I immediately felt uncertain about our exchange. I wondered if he was really attracted to me or simply answering out of convenience. Was I just low-hanging fruit?

Our initial email conversations were short and insignificant. After about a week and a half, Shawn started asking more personal questions, pointing to our potential compatibility, at which point I opened up and things started to get interesting. As our emails grew in length and substance, I began to feel something I hadn't felt in quite some time: hope.

One late night as I lounged around in bed, sipping iced tea while we instant-messaged each other, he asked, "Can I just call you?" Finally. A week of telephone conversations followed, usually before bed. We covered everything from events of the day to our likes, dislikes, hobbies, workout activities, and family dynamics before he asked me, "Can we set a date?" Phew!

Now, as I stand in front of the full-length mirror two days later, I can see that I've executed my strategy perfectly. And, of course, I'm not alone. My old friends, the butterflies (pouncing upon one another in my stomach), are there too. I can't hide my smile. Maybe he's the guy. Maybe . . .

I arrive on time, but Shawn's beaten me to the joint, holding two seats at the end of the long, narrow vintage-style parlor. The club is moody and dark, but he's easy to spot—the only single person in the twelve-seat place. He looks exactly like his photos. Cute. Salt and pepper mixed into his dark-brown hair, unmistakable "I work in the tech industry" black square frames, and signature big smile. He hugs me quickly and smiles more broadly, and I exhale a silent but unexpected burst of air out of my chest. I can breathe a little easier. He likes me and seems happy; I can relax (and try to be myself).

Partway through the evening, I can see he appears to be exactly who he said he was, and there isn't a single "but" in sight. Great guys usually have a "but." You know, he's fantastic but . . .

He's not quite over his ex.

He wants to move to China.

He's quit his job to reinvent himself and isn't sure who he is, where he's going, and what he wants to do yet.

Now the task at hand is to figure out how to keep this initial attraction moving in a positive direction. I know: *I'll be really entertaining*. Story after story, I am, in fact, highly entertaining—for hours. He definitely likes me. He says, "Great atmosphere, delicious drinks, stellar company." He prompts me with questions like, "Do you know of a good interior designer? I could use your help on the house I just renovated." And, "Could you live in two cities? We could spend summers in California and winters in Mexico. You in?" He says, "I admire what you do for a living," and, "My mother would adore you."

Shawn has no idea what he's instigating with this line of conversation. I don't know (yet) that men do this to try ideas on for size, to see how they feel. These seemingly innocuous phrases of plans, promises, and expressions of acceptance and compatibility both set me at ease to be more and more myself and make me like him a wee bit better with every passing word.

As we sit side by side, I can see within the five hours we've spent together that we're a more-than-possible match. This might work. An irresistible combination of smart, kind, and interesting, Shawn seems rare. I appreciate how engaging and playful he is with me. He feels solid and compassionate, funny and sexy. An urbanite living in the most vibrant part of the city, with a life, a real job, and a lot to offer those he cares about. It's as if the Universe has been listening to everything I've ever asked for and wrapped these qualities into the one man placed before me.

Dear God, I know I ask for things all the time, but really, really—just this once—could you make him be the start of something amazing? I'm silently praying in the stall of the ladies' room while I'm on a first date. That isn't weird—is it?

After all, the point is to find my partner. I crave intimacy, growth, and a connection with someone other than my dog. And fine, I'll admit it: I want to do "normal couple things." You know, go out on double dates, host Tuesday taco nights for the gang, sit on his lap in front of a campfire while someone plays guitar and everyone sings badly, go on romantic weekend getaways. Like most women, I long to be cared for, to have a man stroke the side of my face or brush my hair back when it's in my eyes, and whisper into my ear, "I'm the man who loves you."

I don't expect the relationship between Shawn and me to be instantaneous, but I do feel that—I hope that—we're off to a classic start. I know it happens for other people. I've met them.

Near midnight, Shawn asks, "Can I walk you to your car?" Sweet. Our goodnight kiss lasted a little longer than expected, and I'm delighted by what I learn about him in that first kiss.

"Text me when you get home so I know you made it safe," he says, and just like that, I'm hooked. After I send the "I made it home, thank you, goodnight" text, my part is done.

Now I wait.

And wait.

And wait.

Every single hour that passes without the next date on the books makes the critical voice in my head grow louder. Then a full review of the evening begins to play in my brain, and I question everything: *Why did I have to tell that insane story about my family? Did talking about my job scare him away? Was I too flirtatious? Does he think I'm not nurturing enough for his teenage daughter? Was sitting side by side a mistake? Maybe he could see my belly fat.*

With every minute that passes without a text, call, or email, pieces flake off the hunk of hope that once filled my heart. They float to my feet and are crushed as I shuffle through another day.

Shawn is innocent of the cruelty of his simple parting phrases: "I'll call you," and "Let's get together soon."

Inevitably, I face the facts: he was not having the same date I was; there just wasn't enough of a connection for him to want another one. A sense of overwhelming sadness, despair, and loneliness clutters that hopeful space in my heart. I send out an SOS to friends, and they tell me:

"Ah, it was just one date."

"There are plenty of men out there for you!"

"Don't let it get you down. Keep moving; there are plenty more fish in the sea."

"If you date other men right now, you won't be sad about this one."

"He did you a favor by not calling back; that's his polite way of bowing out."

"He must not have been the one for you."

I know this; I've heard it all before. What's worse, I've doled out this same upbeat counsel to my girlfriends and clients countless times. I hate my own advice. I tell myself what I think of my own stupid advice: "Fuck you," I mutter.

Next comes my big choice: I can sit at home and sulk—for days, weeks, months, or, in some of my friends' cases, years—or I can clear it out of my psyche the best I know how and head out there and do it all again: new outfit, new shoes, new mani-pedi, and new guy.

卌   卌   卌

This was simply another false start, and a part of the single person experience. Does it sound familiar?

My friend Leslie says it best: "It's like you've been standing a really, really, really long time, and you see that comfortable chair and it looks so beautiful. You plop down in it, if only for a second, and it's delightful. Soft and warm. It fits your body and brings such relief. You relax. You feel the weight lifted off your feet. You exhale. And before you're anywhere near ready, you're told to get up—it's time to stand again."

For some of us, our response to being hurt is to stop. For good. For others, the idea of dating is so unappealing (or frightening) that we haven't even started.

No longer.

This book is designed to help keep you standing when all you want to do is sit down, even without that comfy chair. You can learn from my (mis)adventures—my experiences on 121 first dates. Whether I wanted to or not, after 121 dates, I'd logged more than enough time to call myself a "dating expert," which I'd never set out to be, by the way. I don't think anyone does. We want to dive in, find our mate, and get the hell out of the dating scene.

There was a light at the end of the dating tunnel because I did meet my guy, but it took 121 dates to get there. And if you're willing, you will find what you're looking for too. I promise to give you solid hope, honest advice, and practical wisdom along with my sometimes terrifying, often hilarious true stories. My dating stories are a tell-all crash course in what real-life dating—with all its ups and downs—can really be like: not perfect or glamorous and not always romantic. Some stories just might curl your hair, others are sure to make you laugh, and maybe one or two will provide a sense of validation of your own experiences. Some of these first dates were fun, insightful, and surprising, and all of them ultimately led me to my partner by helping me understand what it was I was truly looking for.

I want to help you date with the ease and grace I didn't always have. You'll have all that and a bonus: my professional background.

In 2002, after the end of a decade-long marriage and with a heart full of questions, I took part in a workshop through PAX Programs (created by relationship expert Alison Armstrong). My master plan was to understand men better and not make the same mistakes twice. For two days I sat in a hotel conference room with my BFF, Leslie, and thirty women, learning the basics of what I needed to know about men—from a woman. PAX Programs collected the information presented about men, from men. It took a woman I didn't know to illuminate a man's world.

My life was forever altered. I started working for the company immediately, managing and then leading weekend workshops. My new education fueled my endless fascination with men and their points of view. I wanted to know why they do the things they do, and I wanted to experience how understanding what makes men and women different makes our lives so much better.

My relationships with men became more loving and connected after that workshop. I created friendships with men that hadn't been possible before, and I got my feelings hurt less often. It was the beginning of a whole new world and the start of my research. I began by listening to panels of men in workshop rooms I was working in, and it spread to my independent study, which frankly, I can't see ever really ending.

Since 2002 I've conducted social research through interviews with thousands of boys and men ranging in age from eight to eighty-five. I take polls and conduct online surveys. I ask questions of my wide circle of friends and often ask them to ask their friends. I post questions on group discussion boards, asking for public and private feedback, and I have fascinating one-to-one conversations with men on all kinds of topics. My work is never done.

After leading hundreds of workshops to thousands of women on the topics of understanding men, dating, sex, and relationships, I've learned from both men and women the various things we need to create true partnership in our relationships. I offer you the best match possible: personal experience and expertise so that you can trust I've walked my own dating talk. This is, quite literally, my life's work, and I want to share what I've learned with you.

卌   卌   卌

Now let's get back to you. What do you do if you find yourself in a "Shawn" experience or any scenario that doesn't go your way? The answer is never simple, and it's rarely the same from one situation to another. Maybe you're quick to recover and take on new dates right away. Or maybe you opt for a restorative mini break. And let's face it: compared to other dating nightmares, the Shawn date wasn't so horrible, right? Some of us have been burned by this process so many times that we start to resemble blackened toast. That happens from not clearing out the past negative experiences before you're ready to go out and meet someone new.

The last time I found myself in the Shawn scenario, I had to stop. I had to step back, take care of myself, receive nurturing from friends, and know I'd be able to bounce back in what I hoped was a relatively short time. There have also been times when I've been at ninja level, where the overwhelming disappointment of a date has hit me hard, yet I kept going at full speed, still heartbroken but healing myself along the way as best I could and moving through it all because of sheer dating willpower.

So do you keep dating or take a break? Neither choice is wrong. One is not better than the other, and you may find yourself alternating between the two. The key is to take good care of yourself, whatever that looks and feels like for you. Heal (and possibly forgive) yourself and figure out what feels right for you in that moment. You have trustworthy instincts. Use them. This book is designed to help you do exactly that.

There are countless single, available humans on the planet and thousands of different ways to meet them, so you're going to find dates, no doubt. The tricky part is staying in good mental and emotional shape, not dragging past experiences along with you, and hanging in there long enough to find the right person for you. Being willing to experience the Shawn scenario (possibly many Shawn scenarios) and purge it from your system so you can move forward with your heart restored, giving yourself generously to the next one, is all part of dating.

Wherever you're standing now is perfect. You might be just entering the dating scene and experimenting with online dating, or maybe you dated for a while, hated it, gave up, and now you're willing to try again. Maybe you've been dating steadily and you're looking for reassurance, tips, and the resolve to keep going. Wherever you are on your dating trail—at the start or somewhere in the middle—this book will be your personal guide to help you reach your destination. As your trail guide I promise to help steer you clear of low-hanging branches and help you avoid hiking up the steep hard way. I'll even (try to) make you laugh along the way, partly because I think I'm funny and partly because laughing will loosen up the grip of fear and resignation that may be setting in.

My goal is to provide insight into making dating easier for you, and my strategy is persistence. I will offer ways to sort more quickly and keep standing long after you want to give up. I've met many amazing men through dating and using common sense and intuition, and I tested my own dating advice to see what truly works. It paid off in finding my partner. I like to think of myself not so much as lucky as someone who went in with her eyes open, learned from her missteps and the missteps of others, and never gave up.

Please take what resonates with you and leave behind what doesn't. My way (or couple of ways) might not be The One True Way, if there is such a thing. If the shoe doesn't fit for you, it ain't your shoe. Don't cram it on; this could be a long hike. And hey, girl, speaking of "not your shoe," you might not like dating dudes all the time (or at all). Maybe you date women or perhaps you're a bit more free and flexible in your sexual preferences than I am. My experience is one of dating 121 men, but there's *plenty* of good stuff in here for you even if men aren't your thing. So how about this: I'll work in inclusive language where it fits without changing the integrity of my experience and the nature of this book, and you can skip and/or swap out pronouns so the book applies to your life. Deal?

I can't promise that no one will get hurt on the journey, but I'm aiming for fewer scratches and bruises. I'll entertain you while warning of things to look out for, but nothing is 100 percent foolproof, and no way works all the time for every person. Ultimately, go with what works for you and use this book as a guide, not a solution.

Maybe you'll need 121 dates to find your mate, like I did. Or you might hit your jackpot at five. Or twenty. The number isn't the point; what is, is the willingness to put yourself out there despite the uncertainty. Despite the ups and downs. Despite the truckloads of well-meaning but heard-it-all-before advice from friends and family. Despite the really, really, *really* bad dates that can and do happen.

So take a deep breath, crack your knuckles, and remember to treat yourself with kindness. Don't worry; I'll be with you every step of the way.

Part I

~~卌~~ ~~卌~~ ~~卌~~

Getting Ready
to Date

When I was in high school, my home economics teacher always told us, "Measure twice, cut once." This isn't a lesson I took to heart then (as evidenced by the way-too-short shorts and the hideously lopsided pajama pants I ended up with), but it's one I've come to appreciate more and more over the years.

When we decide it's time to dive headfirst into the dating pool, many of us don't take the time to do much planning beforehand. We're excited or scared or worried or an unholy cocktail of all three (throw your arms up if that sounds familiar), and we end up forgetting one of the basic elements of success in any area of life: preparation.

Dating is like anything else in that respect. The more you know before you start, the better off you'll be. That's what I'd like to help you do in this section: be prepared. Prepared for the highs and the lows, the fun bits and the huge bummers, the words of wisdom and the tricks of the trade. I'll take you through the dos and don'ts that have served me and many women in my professional and personal life in navigating the world of dating (online and otherwise) and toss in a couple of hopeful stories and cautionary tales along the way too.

If those 121 first dates I went on taught me anything, it's that being prepared both mentally and physically goes a long way toward making dating efficient, manageable, and, ultimately, successful. Of course, you can't predict everything, especially where intimacy and relationships are concerned, but what you can do is be on your own side. What does that mean? It means that with a little prep work and foresight, you can take care of yourself, be your own champion, and give yourself a bit of a head start before you step out the door to the café around the corner, the local park, or the hot new restaurant in town to meet your potential right match.

Ready to go? Then grab those scissors, but don't snip just yet!

1

What to Expect
(and Not to Expect) from Dating

Here's the truth: You will meet him when you meet him. Period.

This is not a linear process. You could meet him on the first date. That happened for my partner, Dave. I was his first date in twenty-four years. Or you could meet him on the 121st date (that's my story). No one—and I mean no one—can predict how this will work out for you. Trust me, I've paid people to make such predictions.

I know both men and women who signed up online, met their person on their first date, and the two of them live happily ever after. While I'm happy for them, I kinda just want to flick them on the forehead. Expecting that to happen is like an actress expecting to land the lead role on her first audition the day after she moves to Hollywood.

Whoever you are—my curvy or thin sisters, my tall or petite sisters, my white, black, and every-color-in-between sisters, shy or bold, young or old—your happily-ever-after is out there for the taking. The person who's right for you, who will love you for who you are, is out there. You just need to keep standing up and stepping out until the two of you are in front of each other.

Here's my bottom line: when you know how to interact with people with some level of grace and you're fairly sure you can make it through an hour meeting with a total stranger, you're ready to date.

The first thing to know about dating is this: everyone—friends, loved ones, family members, workmates, gym buddies, your Starbucks barista, and every random, well-meaning fuckwit—has an opinion on your dating life (even if it hasn't started yet). Yes, see, they "just know" they have a handle on how you can stop failing and finally get it right.

Once they've learned you're dating (again), it's the hot topic. They have opinions and strategies and well-laid plans they must share with you as if their life depended on it. This will probably annoy the hell out of you. Here's why: They usually share their almost-always-unsolicited strategies with you *after* you've experienced something miserable in your dating life. This is when they spring into action (like the world's most well-intentioned but incompetent superhero), giving you tips on how to date the "correct way," because clearly you're doing it all wrong. Never mind that they weren't there with you and don't know the whole story—I mean, who needs facts, anyway? Face it, you're *this* close to being a tragic loner, and they don't want that for you. They want to save you. They'll tell you all kinds of "helpful" things—lines like, "They'll show up when you least expect it."

Really? I had a decade of not yet having my partner, and believe me, there were multiple months where I "least expected" it. I know dozens if not *hundreds* of single women who never expect it, and guess what: it hasn't happened for them (yet), either.

"You've got to make it a full-time job. Put some effort into it."

Wow, really? Dating doesn't pay the rent, my friends!

"Don't try so hard."

Uh, I thought you wanted me to put some effort into it?

"Your bar is set too high."

Seriously? Expecting a decent, civilized conversation over a glass of iced tea with someone is setting the bar too high?

As you'll learn later on, I'm wary of dating strategies. If you choose to follow one and it works, then I say (and mean) good for you. Unfortunately, the majority of what I see when women adopt one strategic dating method or another is a lot of women doing a lot of work, following exercises and dating plans trying to reel in the right partner. Working hard for what you want is good and all, but when he doesn't show up after all that effort, these women tend to blame themselves and not the strategy for being deficient.

Strategy or no strategy, how you dive into (or back into) the dating scene will have much to do with what you expect from the whole process.

So what are you expecting from your first date?

Are you setting the bar too high?

Will you hope to yank your online dating profile down within the first five minutes of meeting your date?

Are you praying he wants to have six children too?

Whether it's a blind date, an online date, or a first date with someone you met on a night out, you should have one expectation for the first date: that you both make it through with ease, grace, and in kindness to each other. You can't expect to know if your date likes you as much as you like him. Oftentimes he will tell you, which is sweet, but not always.

You can't expect to know the truth about his intentions with you. I don't mean that your date is a liar—I don't mean that at all. But both men and women often quickly make up their mind about whether or not they are going to see their date again, and out of what they perceive as kindness, they don't share that information while on the date. They think they're being nice or polite and socially graceful. How misguided they are. Who hasn't kept mum in person to spare a date's feelings until they could shoot off an email or text or private message instead? It may feel easier, but it's rarely the better option.

While you don't owe your first date anything, it's genuinely kind and gracious to tell the truth. In person. When asked, "Can I call you tomorrow?" if you're not feeling it, please don't say yes. Women do this all the time. It's the top complaint I hear from men. But for anyone who truly wants to see the other person again, it's aggravating to read a false positive.

Instead, be honest. Say something like, "Thanks so much for offering to call. I don't think we're quite a match. I wish you luck out there."

You know how discouraging it is when you've had an amazing date and you wait for that call, only to discover after a week that it's not coming? Yeah, don't be that person.

So what else can you expect from dating?

Expect to meet people.

Expect to ask and answer questions that are uplifting, fun, or bring out the unique sides of each other.

Expect that there may not be chemistry—for you, for him, for either one of you. No chemistry happens often.

Strive for bringing out the best in him by having him talk about what he cares about.

Strive for learning something new about this person.

Strive for being heard and understood concerning things that are important to you.

Strive for a friendly, connected, fun time that could lead to more friendly, connected, fun times.

Strive for being honest when it's time to let each other know where you are on this date. Do you want off the ride? Or do you want to keep going? This may include a change of venues on the same night. Say you're having fun at dinner and he offers a stroll, a dessert somewhere else, or a drink at a favorite wine bar; if you're having fun, then simply say yes. If you're done, don't drag the date on just to be pleasant. End it.

There may be times when you know you're never going to see each other again but you're having a good time. In this case you can continue; just be conscious that you're not leading him on throughout the date.

Date #44
Bison and a Massage—
What's Not to Love?

Setting: Iced tea at the Depot Bookstore & Café, Mill Valley, CA

I stood in line at the Depot—a cool, old California Mission–style landmark building in the center of Mill Valley's downtown. Once a train station for mill workers, its current function is churning out espresso and croissants and offering a meeting place for singles like me. As I lingered and looked around, waiting my turn to order iced tea, I spotted my date standing in line behind me.

Even though we hadn't yet introduced ourselves, I knew he was not my man. I think he knew it too, because from the start of the date he pushed a hard sales pitch: He focused on his philanthropic endeavors, including saving people, the planet, and animals.

"Animals?"

"I save all kinds of large animals and help relocate them to sanctuaries and the private sector around the Bay Area, mostly in Marin," he said, "like bison."

"Bison? SHOW ME!" I exclaimed, too intrigued to not blurt out the request (or, rather, the demand).

"Really?" he said with hope.

"Yes!"

We made our way through the long, steady coffee line, grabbed our drinks, and sat down at a tiny, round granite café table so small that it was better suited for one.

"So if you want to see the bison, I need to know what your time-line is today," he said.

"My plan is to have coffee with you and then head to a massage appointment in a little under two hours. So we have a little time," I replied.

"Do you think you can get me in for a massage appointment too?" he asked.

"Sure," I answered as I punched in #7 on my cell phone, the speed dial to the spa.

Next thing you know, this man (who I had no interest in ever seeing again) and I were in my secondhand BMW convertible, top down, driving to Nicasio on a warm summer day to visit bison on an estate with vast acreage. When we arrived at the private gate, it took him more than a few guesses to punch in the right code. I felt the tingling excitement of being a trespasser, which I'm sure we were. Eventually—voilà—the gate swung open, and over the hill the bison were there to greet us. Oh, they were cute—wooly, substantial in size, bigger than I'd expected.

While the bison appeared completely disinterested in our arrival, I was thrilled. I took my time, saying hi to each and every massive bison. The brown ones, the darker brown one, the creamy one—dozens of them, all with horns on their head so large I couldn't imagine them not being burdened by their weight and size. I had lengthy one-way conversations with each of them, eyeball to eyeball. I informed them of their cuteness, questioned them about their potential balance problems due to their horns, asked how they were eating. I didn't get much of a response from any of them, but I didn't mind. All this was taking place while my date pondered how exactly he was going to pry me off the fence so we could make it back to town in time for our massages.

He managed to find the right words because eventually I gave in, sad to leave my new bison friends much sooner than I would have liked. I drove about ten miles over the speed limit the whole way back, just so we could make our appointment (oops). The staff at the hippie massage retreat in the redwoods were ready for our ninety-minute massages—in separate rooms, of course. Afterward, pummeled nearly speechless and dizzy with bodily bliss, we met in the front reception room to pay our bill and say our few words of good-bye.

$$\text{卌} \qquad \text{卌} \qquad \text{卌}$$

What I think I did right on the bison date: I had an incredibly fun and memorable day with a total stranger, while kindly letting him know this was a "friend" thing and we wouldn't be dating. Sure, moments of it were slightly uncomfortable, like mid-date when he asked when he could see me again. I said in my friendliest and most sincere tone, "I am having a fun day with you. The bison were a crack-up, and the spa is going to feel amazing. But I don't think you and I are quite right for each other. This is our last date, but I hope we can enjoy today."

He seemed amiable and not at all surprised. I didn't want to do to him what had been done to me time and again. It's cruel to let your date think you're feeling it right up to the end. I despise the rug pull.

I did good (this time).

2

Getting Ready for Your Dating Adventure

Taking excellent care of yourself is critical for attracting a suitable match and maintaining your sanity. Desperation isn't charming or attractive. No one wears it well, and you don't want to work yourself into a state so crazed that you settle for the first warm body you come across simply because he's within arm's reach.

You can bring yourself to remarkable shape if you can identify these two things: what you need and what makes you happy. Let's jump right in!

Start by making two lists. Label the top of the first page "NEED" and the top of the second page "HAPPY."

Need

Most think there should only be three words on the NEED list: food, water, and shelter. But for the sake of being in top dating shape, let's look beyond that. Sure, you could say you're low-maintenance, that you don't really need anything. Just like a car doesn't need gas or oil. Hell, it doesn't even need wheels . . . if it's sitting on blocks in someone's side yard. In order to perform well and go anywhere at all, you're going to need a bit of TLC.

Things you need are generally things that, when you go without them, you feel upset, off balance, or unwell. You're not your best self. You are not fine. Other emotions you might experience when you don't have what you need are irritation or frustration. For example, I need eight hours of sleep a night on a regular basis. If I'm only sleeping five or six hours for several nights in a row, I'm cranky and off balance. I need walks in nature at least once a week. Without them I'm tense and tightly wound. I need eleven minutes of daily meditation in the morning. Without it I feel off-kilter, off purpose, and often not that productive. I need mommy time with my dog every day. Without the ability to love her up and nurture her I feel lonely and slightly disconnected, and it takes me longer to access genuine affinity for pretty much anyone. In other words, my dog makes me a better human, so not only do I need that connection but so does everyone else around me.

Happy

Once you've got what you need and you're well, look at what would make life even better. What makes you happy? Sleeping in makes me happy. Going to the cinema to see a film that will sweep me away makes me happy. Chocolate-covered apricots make me happy. I don't *need* any of what I've listed (because I'm well without them), but they're delightful—they're the bonuses in life.

So what are you going to do with these lists? You're going to start them, add to them, and keep them posted on your fridge. Carry them around until you know them so well you don't need the physical paper anymore. Especially for the things you need, be specific. If you wrote down, "Time with my girlfriends," how much time? Alone time, physical time, what's enough (the minimum per day, week, or month) to get you to well? I want you in good shape.

But why is being well important?

When you're well, you have everything you need. You're not upset or off balance, trying to be amazing on top of not being well. We have a tendency to spend too much time trying to be amazing when we're not okay. We try to be happy even when our minimal needs haven't been met, and the experience is similar to eating ice cream on an empty stomach: it's nauseating. If we spent most of our time focused on getting ourselves to well, the world would be a completely different (and much lovelier) place.

On the one hand, our culture likes to tell us that, as women, we deserve and should have it all. On the other, it also likes to suggest that a good woman is completely selfless and low maintenance. It's frustrating and confusing. Many of us think that low maintenance is what men are looking for in a woman, right? Wrong. I'm not suggesting you go into full diva mode, either. The trick, as with most things, is balance. To keep yourself running in top shape, know what you need and what makes you happy, and implement accordingly. Teach yourself how to express this to people. (Hint: Be direct and use the words "need" and "happy.") People look for and need that information from you.

I can't stress this enough: If you want to run like a Ferrari at optimum levels, you're not going to try to get by on discount fuel. You need some things. You can be high maintenance if you're also high performance, and you can speak to what you need without being demanding, expectant, or entitled.

As a single girl, I came up with things I could do for myself that would bring me to well *and* make me happy. I'm responsible for my own self-care. Doing these things for yourself helps keep you in top shape mentally, emotionally, and physically and can help you avoid feeling so hungry or empty or lonely when the dating blues set in (which, despite our best efforts, they do from time to time).

To help you start your own self-care list, here are a few things I did for myself.

Get a Massage

Once a week, once a month, once a quarter—whatever you can afford—get a massage, if that's something that nurtures you.

When the economy was better, I got a ninety-minute massage every Friday. When the economy was terrible, I hit the inexpensive foot massage place for a twenty-minute treatment every now and again.

Whether it was every Friday or a random splurge, I asked for a male provider. Having a man do bodywork made all the difference. Pick the gender you want touching you. It's therapeutic, connective, and rejuvenating. Having a professional caretake your body will nurture and feed you in ways you miss when you're going without physical intimacy in your life.

Buy Yourself Flowers

Do you daydream about your beloved bringing you your favorite flowers? Are they red roses? You can buy a dozen red roses at the grocery store any day of the week for about ten bucks, except for right around Valentine's Day. I'd pick up two dozen red roses on Friday mornings so they'd be fresh at the start of my weekend. With self-love, it's important to respect how much you might need, even if an inner voice tells you it's excessive. Don't underestimate the power and impact of two dozen red roses on your state of mind.

I share this tip when I lead my eight-week dating tele-class. Once in a later session, a woman raised her hand and said, "I did it! I went out and bought myself flowers just like Wendy said. I did it because I had just learned that the man I was dating wasn't going to ask me out for the weekend, and I'd secretly saved my time for him. I have to say, I put them in a vase and for the rest of the weekend, whenever I looked at those flowers I was so happy."

When a suitor who wants to impress you comes over and sees two dozen gorgeous roses taking up half your desk, he'll know exactly what makes you happy and what to bring you the next time he shows up. Want to know what to say when asked about the roses? Tell the truth. "I love red roses. I buy them because they make me happy."

Note: That right there is an example of how to tell somebody what makes you happy.

Eat Yummy Food

Even if it's just takeout from your favorite spot, treat yourself. If you reserve food you enjoy only for special occasions like dating, you'll feel wanting and hungry for more than just food.

Waiting around for someone to offer to take you to your favorite restaurant is lame. Dress yourself up, take yourself out. Sit at the bar while sipping a luscious drink, and savor every bite of your meal. Don't deprive yourself of the decadence. Besides, while you're indulging yourself with food and ambiance, you could smile and say hi to the cute customer sitting next to you.

Have Sex

You heard me. Have sex! You can adopt a lover or a friend with benefits, or you can have sex on your own through masturbation. I have much more to say on both these topics, but I think you need a bit more foreplay from me before we go there, so keep reading.

Having sex may be on the NEED side of your list. (It's on mine.) Having the sex you need keeps you from being too hungry on your dates—so hungry that you end up being unable to wait for the right time to have sex for the first time.

Nurture Your Sensuality

Dance. Awaken your feminine body movement. Dancing is fun (says the girl who won't dance in public unless there's a pole involved). Dance in your room to your favorite pop singer. Take ballet, tango, salsa, hip-hop, or pole-dancing classes. Don't pick one simply because it seems challenging; you already have enough challenging things in your life. Pick the one that feels like it would be the most fun.

I never liked dancing. I always felt uncoordinated and dorky. Then I found pole dancing and I fell in love. I'm not saying you should do it or love it, and it's not for everyone. What is for every woman is dancing in a way that can put you in touch with your feminine self. I get this from pole dancing and nowhere else. I promote what Sheila Kelley, founder of the S Factor pole dancing studios, refers to as finding and bringing out your "erotic creature."[1] You can nurture your femininity (your primal feminine self living deep inside you), and you can draw her out by dancing s-l-o-w. In your own bedroom, lights off, candles lit, lean your back against an empty wall and sway your hips to a slow-moving song that makes you feel sexy. Turn the music up and just check out. Let your erotic creature move to the music for you; let her tell you what she wants. She'll come out if you let her.

You might find out you have a sexual, sensual side that's nothing like your everyday personality. You might never have even met this creature before. She may be dark. She may be playful. She may like things you don't like. She is a creature unto herself.

Strangely enough, my erotic creature is shy. As you might imagine, I'm not a shy person. She likes scarves, boas, and ties around her neck, while I can't stand to wear anything tight around my neck in my daily life. My point is this: Even if she seems contradictory or a bit weird, nurture her, call her out, let her dance. Let her show you the sensual power living inside you.

So move and grind to your favorite slow songs. Do it in half time. I double-dog dare you. If you take this on and feel like you might just have stumbled upon something (like the holy grail of your sensuality, femininity, and womanhood), dig in a little further by spending twenty minutes in front of YouTube watching "Let's Get Naked: Sheila Kelley at TEDxAmericanRiviera."[2] It's a TED talk that every woman needs to watch.

There's another reason to nurture your sensuality, and that's for those you date. It's easy to go from work-and-task mode—being 105 percent "on," multitasking, organizing our to-do lists, and producing all those serious results—to date mode without actually leaving your work self at the office. You find yourself sitting down to dinner and drinks like you're with a client, not with a potential match, and trust me, sister, this is not sexy. For the good of everyone involved, you need to take a moment to shift, and the fastest way to shift is to tap into your softer, more sensual side by dancing, moving, singing, and slowing down.

Nurture Your Serenity

Find peace in the forest or along a deserted beach. Walk your favorite canyon or hike that regional park you've been meaning to check out. Even city dwellers have access to a large park somewhere relatively nearby. Find the time—even if it's only thirty minutes—to breathe fresh air and regain some balance in nature. It will give you a broader perspective and answers to questions you've been struggling with all week.

Take a long, luxurious bath with salts, bubbles, or oils. Listen to music, light some candles, and make it a ritual.

Read—and I don't mean reports or trade magazines. Whether it's romance or adventure, be captivated by a world outside your own.

Meditate in a quiet place; start by expressing gratitude.

Invite Men into Your Life

Let men be kind to you, open doors for you, flirt with you, buy you lunch when you're down in the dumps. You know the ones. The ones who love you just as you are.

Let him tell you all the amazing things about you when you most need to hear it. Let those words move beyond your ears and wash over your heart.

Cultivate close male friendships. Clear, conscious, nonsexual, real friendships. These friendships are priceless. You can call on your go-to guy when you need a man's perspective on something, a shoulder to cry on, or to hear from a man about how brilliant, beautiful, and essential you are.

Sometimes your main guy is busy, so bring in more than one. Add new men to your friend tree. When you're single, it takes a village to keep you in top shape, and that village should definitely include guys.

Nurture Love in Your Life

Spend focused "love" time with your dog, your cat, your pot-bellied pig, a close friend, or a family member. Let them contribute and acknowledge their love for you. If you don't have a pet, close friends, or family nearby, volunteer at a local animal shelter or sanctuary where your gift of love can make a difference.

Get It from a Stranger

What? A stranger? Yes, receive love from a stranger. Especially if you work from home or spend a lot of time isolated from others. Go out into the world and connect with the people you pass on the street. Smile or send them love and receive it in turn.

My bestie, Leslie, stayed single for a long time. When I voiced concern about her happiness, she said, "I'm in good shape. I don't need a boyfriend right now. I have hundreds of them right outside my front door." And she was right. She received compliments, smiles, and offers of help from nearly every man she saw each day. Whether it was her neighbor offering to shovel snow off her walkway or the market clerk joking around with her and making special recommendations, she enjoyed their generosity and happily received their attention. It made her feel appreciated, loved, and connected to men everywhere.

Men are dying to say hello to you. They want to see your smile. Most of them don't want anything more from you than that— acknowledgment of their appreciation of your beauty, for that connection. This doesn't mean you should strike up conversations with every catcaller on the sidewalk; it's more about that mutual, if fleeting, appreciation between the sexes that can happen every day in the smallest of ways if you're open to it. So if you're in the mood, go ahead, give a brother what he's after—your authentic radiance. It can make his day and can even change your life.

Use the Buddy System

Make a deal with a girlfriend or two (or a guy friend or two) to help you through this phase of your life. Better that she or he be in the same boat so you can reciprocate, and the two of you will have a mutual understanding of what you're going through. (A note on married folk: Often married people can't relate. They either haven't experienced this phase because they didn't date much before they got hitched or have forgotten what it was like [like the pain of childbirth]. How quickly the experience fades once you find your match and slip into the bliss of a daily routine as a couple!)

Think of these single friends as your dating allies. Dating allies are there to listen. You know how valuable a patient girlfriend can be.

She can take in twenty minutes of content without uttering a word (as if she could get one in in the first place). Set up your ally or allies to listen to all the details—the good, the bad, and the ugly—so you can be free of them.

I've found that once I've told someone my story, I feel much better. The upset is not living inside my body anymore; it's out. Find your magic number of allies—whether it's just your closest pal or a group of friends—and line up enough support to spill the details without scaring everyone off. It's a balance.

Give your dating buddy permission to be straight with you. I had several throughout my dating experience, and my friend and dating supporter, who we'll call "Seattle Nate," was the one who often told me it was time for a break from dating. He'd hold me accountable for coming back when I was ready. Here's what that looked like.

Date #83
Hit the Wall

Setting: Tea at Starbucks, Marin County

"I'm on my way to this one now. Seventeen more dates and I reach one hundred—and frankly, my dear, I don't give a damn," I groused through my car's speakerphone as I sat in evening traffic.

Seattle Nate listened and generously said, "My love, I've never run a marathon, but I hear one hits a wall somewhere between eighteen and twenty miles. You have hit the wall. I feel sorry for all of them—this one and the sixteen you've got left after him. So . . . after you bang them out, what's next?"

"I quit. I'm out. Walk the dog. Maybe learn how to play piano, write a book, or ride a horse. I'll wear muumuus 24/7."

He plays along because he's kind that way. "I think taking a photography or painting class may be a better way to take care of yourself while you're taking a break, Wendy."

Take a break? I both appreciate and resent the voice of reason.

My date turns out to be a nice person. Our date, as it happens, is his first Match.com date ever. Aww, he's a virgin. I did not tell him he was Date #83.

Date #83 is a trial attorney and a natural storyteller. He's charming, says all the right things to me, and wants to do it again. Okay. Then he says, "I'm in the middle of a messy divorce."

"And you're looking to get out of something, not into something, right?"

"Well . . . I want to date you, but I thought it was only fair to tell you."

"Uh-huh . . ." I nodded, searching for something—anything—to say. I was just so tired. "Well, I'm uncomplicated. That might be refreshing for you," I said. What I really wanted to say was, *Don't worry; you don't need to explain, because I no longer care.*

ʇʜʟ   ʇʜʟ   ʇʜʟ

So what happened?

I took a break, and about ten dates later it was time for another break. Seattle Nate said, "I know you. You're an *amazing* partner. But even if you met an exceptional match right now, Wendy, he wouldn't see you. He wouldn't see you. He'd see a crunchy, crabby, bitter, deflated version of what used to be you." He was right.

Your dating buddy can help you tell when it's time to stop dating and when it's time to start again. After all, you've only quit temporarily for realignment and self-care; you're not quitting until you're perfectly happy or just for the sake of quitting, right?

What dating allies are *not* good for: explaining why a man did what he did. Your friend doesn't know why the guy didn't call. She also can't interpret what he meant by his silence. Please don't ask her, because she'll tell you, but not from a man's point of view and certainly not from his point of view. Each person's motivations, reasons, expressions, and answers are going to be different from another's. You want to know why a person did something? Ask him. If you can't, you need to go by what they said about it and leave it at that. It's healthier, it's saner, and in the long run it's gonna save you a lot of grief and handwringing.

Even though they can't give you all the answers, never underestimate the power of your dating allies. You need them to debrief "what happened" so they can love you up and reassure you that you did nothing wrong.

A quick note before we continue: Many of my 121 first dates were some flavor of fun, fantastic, hopeful, and connective with nice, respectable, wonderful men. They aren't like the one you're going to read about next. Here's a fine example of a date gone bad. Enjoy.

Date #109
Drive-by

Setting: A regional park, Oakland, CA

This online connection moved to the telephone to in person within two days. The plan was a date to walk our dogs.

I was aiming for a serene hike in my favorite regional park filled with mossy oaks, manzanitas, madrones, and trails boasting views of vineyard hillsides in Glen Ellen, California. If I threw a blanket in the back of the car and made a quick stop at the Community Café in Sonoma to pick up a gourmet picnic lunch (peanut butter-and-chocolate-dipped marshmallow treats included), this could have been an ideal first meeting that would lead to a hopeful happily ever after. He had other plans.

"Hey, there's a park right by my house," he said. "Come on down and we'll walk the Oakland/Alameda shoreline."

"Okay, how do I get there?" I asked.

While he provided directions, I could picture the area. As I recalled the landmarks and cross streets, it registered as a sketchy, concrete-laden industrial area in a rough part of Oakland. We would definitely not be enjoying the expansive views and natural beauty of the wine country.

"Okay, that could work. What time do you want me there?" I asked.

"Three. I'll see you there."

We arrived—"we" meaning me and Lilly-Bee, my medium-sized Catahoula Leopard dog. She's kind of a badass and definitely my protector, so we didn't worry too much about the location, despite the fact that getting there required that I drive on unmaintained alleyways past abandoned and vandalized factories in Oakland (and I'm talking about the ten-o'clock-news Oakland, not the hills or the north side of town).

We pulled into the lot and were ready to get our date on at 2:50. Lilly-Bee and I were the only two in the parking lot.

So we waited.

And waited.

And waited.

By 3:10 we were restless, so we began to roam around the area near the parking lot.

We waited. And waited. And waited some more.

At 3:18 we spotted a beat-up and rusted green Dodge Dart with massive amounts of blue duct tape plastered against the full length of the front of the car just to hold the frame together. As it pulled closer, a cattle doggie popped her head out the back driver's-side window.

I waved, smiled, and waited. The engine of the car continued to run. Okay.

I walked over to the driver's side. His window was down. I mustered up a friendly "Hi."

"Hey," he responded. "Um . . . so . . ."

(Pause.)

"Umm . . . uh, I cut my foot. I think I need to drive home to bandage it up."

"Okay," I replied.

"I'll call you later to reschedule," he lied, and drove off.

           ‖‖   ‖‖   ‖‖

As he drove away, leaving me standing in an ugly, isolated parking lot, I realized this whole maneuver was most likely intentional. From the abandoned meeting place to being late, he set the date up so he could drive by to see if I was worthy of his time but without having the guts to deal with any incompatibility head-on and with some tact. In my humble opinion, this was a cowardly, douchebag move.

This is where your dating ally comes in. Thankfully, I was able to reach Leslie on the phone and share the whole story. She asked, "Are you still in your walking shoes?"

"Yes," I replied.

"Got your headset on?"

"Yep."

"Okay, then grab the dog and let's go. Why don't we walk your favorite loop heading east from your house?"

Still in my walking shoes, I took Lilly-Bee for that hike I'd promised her earlier, and Leslie (via cell phone) came with us, making up hilarious, alternative stories about what really might have happened with this guy.

I laughed the whole way.

Hot Tip Meet your date in a safe, well-lit, well-trafficked public area where you'll be comfortable and at ease. You'll have a better shot at showing up as your best self when you're not off-balance. If you're going on a nature hike, make sure you're meeting in a place so filled with beauty there will be dozens upon dozens of people nearby. In other words, have better common sense than I did on this date.

3

Dos and Don'ts Before the First Date

During my time as a dating, sex, and relationship expert and over the course of my personal dating adventures, I've learned that we women pay attention to many things at once. We focus on our career and what we're building there. We tend to our relationships with friends and family. We volunteer in our communities. What's missing from this list so far? Ding ding ding! Paying attention to ourselves.

Forgetting to take care of yourself can be easy to do when living a fast-paced, multitasking life—particularly in terms of one's dating life. For example, many of us tend to put little or no thought into what we do (or don't do) before a first date. How you care for yourself before your date can have a direct impact on the success of that date.

There are certain facts about modern life that we just can't escape: We are busy, and most of us hardly ever get enough rest. We don't plan time or give ourselves any space between activities. We run from one appointment to the next, including dates, making the date one more thing on an already full to-do list.

I once scheduled a date for 9:00 PM when my workday had started at 4:30 AM. It was my first day on a new job that required a drive totaling two hundred miles round-trip. It had been a full day of work, during which I was introduced to my new team and had to make executive decisions that affected the next calendar year. I met my date after that workday, on my drive home. Ridiculous.

We schedule dates right after work without giving ourselves any time to stop being in go-go-go mode, and this is a mistake.

Your date wants to be with a woman who is relaxed, comfortable in her own skin, chill, and happy. You're none of these things when you rush to your date after a full day of work. While you may have changed your clothes, you still show up in your career-oriented energy, ready to produce that next result—in this case, conquering a date. As hard as you try, a goal-led persona is rarely of particular appeal to anyone on a date.

Give yourself enough time to be present, relaxed, and able to give your best first impression. If possible, avoid meeting a date right after work or another obligation. Don't meet after you've spent the day with your friends (unless they're helping you prepare for the evening); you've already given your best to them.

I recommend taking at least an hour to transition away from your stressful day before a date. Take a bubble bath or throw Epsom salts in the tub to wash off your day. Breathe, meditate, or grab a ten-minute disco nap. Take your time glamming yourself up. Choose jewelry or an outfit that is an expression of your unique style. Use the "getting ready" process as a ritual to appreciate yourself. Dress up with something pleasing to you, such as a flirty bracelet, your favorite earrings, or a special item you don't normally wear.

The exception: I'd say only go directly to a date after you've done something physical, such as yoga or a dance class. These activities put you in your body, bring you to your core self, and bring forth your unique sensual femininity—what could be yummier than that? But don't wear your yoga pants—unless, of course, that's what you wear 24/7, in which case, you rock 'em, sistah.

Speaking of R&R . . . masturbate. That is, if you want to purposely cause sexual attraction. On another note, can you believe I'm whipping out masturbation already? Yep, I am, because I've got critical information about masturbation. If you do it before a date, you will cause a stirring within and some very predictable responses will occur. Let's take a look at the cause and effect so you hold all the power.

You'll become sexually aroused (duh), which will draw out your sensual side and get you in touch with your body. You will show up to the date feeling naturally sexy, feminine, and ready to connect (compliments of the bonding hormone, oxytocin).

The effects of masturbation will act on more than just your brain and your uterus and will linger around your body for hours, even all day and into the night. Let me break it down for you: The positive emotional state is associated with increased dopamine and opioid peptide activity in your reward circuits (we're talking biology here). The hypothalamus floods your body with oxytocin, causing uterine contractions that generate orgasm sensations. It's not just about the physical, however. Oxytocin, aka the "love and bonding hormone," then hangs out in your system and looks for bonding opportunities. That's its whole job, to bond—and it's looking for a partner to bond to. As the nucleus accumbens, or "pleasure center," receives dopamine, you, my friend, are higher than high. If you'd like to learn more about this sort of thing, check out the work of behavioral neuroscientist Barry R. Komisaruk, PhD, who leads MRI studies on women's orgasms (a kind of weird and potentially awesome job, if you ask me).[3]

So there you are, all zingy. Your date senses it, it activates desire, and we've now jump-started sexual attraction.

Good news, right? Maybe. Knowing about this will help you choose when you're going to use this tool to your benefit and understand the response you may get from a date when it's used to your detriment. When we feel strong sexual attraction, we can inadvertently end up with a booty call. If that's something you aren't looking for, you may want to be mindful of this, especially before your first date. Of course, if you do want a hookup, then go get it!

Understand that if you masturbate before your date (not *in front of* your date; that's a whole different thing), you have a high likelihood of causing sexual attraction, which can be a delicious thing. But if you're looking for a partner (versus a hookup), you want your date to be both sexually attracted to you and to appreciate much more about you than just your physicality. You want him to enjoy your stellar personality and see that you're funny, smart, and totally amazing, and a person not worth jeopardizing by making a fumble such as trying to bed you the first night. I'm guessing you want him to feel compelled to see you again, look out for what you need, and figure out how he can make you happy. When sexual attraction is intense, it can be hard to focus on anything else, let alone anything long-term. The adage "he's just got one thing on his mind" has a point in this particular situation. And while I know plenty of people (including me) who've had deep, meaningful relationships and marriages with mates after sleeping with them on the first date, it's not a strategy I offer to you as a slam-dunk way to catch your mate.

The next date story is a stellar example of a first date with too much sexual energy.

Date #98
Warning: X-Rated

Setting: A progressive date starting with dinner at Izzy's Steakhouse, San Francisco, CA

Let's start with the disclaimer, shall we? I recommend you skip this vignette if you're my mother, my Mormon paternal grandparents, or the like. Those of you who prefer your reading to stay safely in PG-13 territory may also want to take a pass. For those of you reading on, buckle up.

Date #98 had contacted me a few weeks earlier, but days before we were to meet, a dog bit me on the face. The bite required eight stitches right below my right eye. I wasn't up for seeing anyone new.

He wanted to meet before the stitches came out, which made me love him just a little bit, but I had to say, "No way!" I was willing to let him see a cool-looking scar but not eight black whiskers woven between clumps of blood with scabs poking out of my face.

One of the things that attracted me to him was his life's work. He was the executive director for a nonprofit organization in San Francisco representing a cause dear to my heart. He seemed to be the type of man I could get behind and support. But at Date #98, the skeptic in me didn't bother with excitement until we actually met face-to-healing-face.

On the date, I discovered he was intelligent and interesting but not particularly funny and not at all my type, yet I wanted to give him a chance.

Over three hours of dinner conversation, his top two hot topics were his ex-wife and his ex-girlfriend. From what I gathered, there was quite a bit of overlap.

By the conclusion of dinner, I'd learned which of my body parts were his favorites (and neither of them happened to be my brain). "I want to date you," he said, "but I have a feeling you're a real prude." Huh. Cue to watch the date go sideways. I was insulted, and my mind flooded with rhetorical questions I never asked him but will ask you:

1. Uh, what's prudish about a short black skirt, knee-high boots with six-inch heels, and a cleavage-showing top?

2. Why does it make me a prude if I won't act overtly sexual on a first date?
3. Why was my "prudishness" pushed on me like a deal-breaking character flaw or a permanent badge?

Needless to say, this date was officially over. I thanked him for the meal and said, "This prude has to go dance at a club now."

"Where?"

"Never you mind," I said.

"Can I come watch?"

I thought about it. "Only if we take separate cars. You can come, I guess. The club doesn't open for another hour an a half."

"We could go for a drink," he said.

"Fine, but only if we go to Aunt Charlie's," I replied. Aunt Charlie's is this magnificent teeny-tiny hole-in-the-wall dive bar that caters to the LGBT crowd and features drag queen revues on weekends. It's awesome.

I arrived after my date and found him sitting at the far end of the bar. Between us was a group of eight to ten gay men in their late twenties and early thirties. I pushed my way past the boys and joined Date #98 for a quick beer while we waited.

The berating of my character due to the "prude flaw" continued. He pulled at my blouse to show me how I should wear it if I weren't so prudish, and as he tugged, the top of the center of my blouse fell well below my bra. I'd had it with this guy. I turned around to my crowd of boys (decorative bra showing and all) and announced, "It's time for a poll. How many of you"—I raised my hand high in the air—"think I'm a prude?"

Cutie pie #1, in his queenliest voice, said, "Honey. In those boots? You are NOT a prude!"

The others quickly followed suit, commenting on my bra, my skirt, and my being at Aunt Charlie's in the middle of the Tenderloin, one of San Francisco's seediest neighborhoods. Yes, it was well documented; the votes were cast, and the committee ruled that I was (shocker) *not* a prude. With that, I said, "Thank you, my friends. Now this prude has to excuse herself. She's got to go dance on a pole at the Power Exchange."

Something to know about me that you've probably picked up on by now: for recreation and elation, I dance on a pole. Yep, I'm a pole dancer. I'm amazing at it. I can climb, flip, spin, and more. I'm better than most of the "professionals."

But back to the date. I'll explain the Power Exchange. You might guess it's a bar. It's not. Strip club? Nope. Give up?

The Power Exchange is a sex club as well as one of San Francisco's only safe havens for transgender women to safely play. I love this place.

The central area of this club, which I like to call the living room, just so happens to be home to San Francisco's best pole available to the public. It's in the center of the room at the end of a long professional runway stage that's underlit.

I like to dance there on occasion. I dive in during the off-hours when no one is around but staff, who are fantastic, by the way. They're similar to bartenders and bouncers, and you just know they've seen every single thing under the sun. They're jaded but friendly, and they like me because I'm friendly back.

Remember keg parties in college? Kids may have been kissing in the living room but the real action always played out in the back bedrooms (or so we see in John Hughes films). Well . . . it's like that in this club. Center stage is me on a pole (if I'm not dancing, I'm giving another woman a pole lesson), and whatever else the central space has got going on is usually some sort of deal-making session or transaction. In other words, the living room is mostly talk, not a lot of action, not at the nine o'clock hour, anyway. One might see people trying to work out the deal of a threesome or trying to coordinate potential play. I don't listen in; it's not my business. I focus on the pole.

This night I walked in, greeted my friends behind the counter, and headed into the living room toward the stage with the man formerly known as my "date" trailing behind me. Two women in their mid-twenties—hipster-vintage-Goth types—leapt up and squealed when they saw me. "Our favorite pole dancer. Yay!" I gave them each a big hug and then hauled one of the girlies on stage with me. We worked out some easy spinning tricks as a warm-up. She was a big girl and shy about using her full body weight on the pole, so I worked with her for a while. I taught; we spun; I danced. My life was perfect.

About thirty minutes into dancing, I found myself about fifteen feet up in the air, inadvertently looking eye level at someone in the second-story seating gallery. When I realized he'd caught my eye, I quickly looked away. I actually make it a point not to look at men in the club because I don't want to accidentally start something I have zero intention of finishing with them. It's just protocol.

So while I was dangling fifteen feet in the air—upside down, mind you—I averted my eyes to somewhere safe. Normally, that would be down at the empty stage below me. This time I chose to look over to my group of girls and my ex-date.

The women were gone; it was only my ex-date. Naked. Completely naked (even his shoes and socks were off) and looking up at me . . . and masturbating.

All I could think was, dude, it's the living room. I know it's allowed and all, but it's not cool. Put your shoes on, at least—that's unsanitary—and if that's for me, I'd like you to put that thing away or take it to the back room away from me. *Apparently I proved his point*, I thought, laughing internally. *I am a prude.*

I lingered in the air as long as possible but eventually popped down off the pole, at which time I grabbed my bag off the stage and proceeded to leave.

"Wait!" he called out, erection in hand like he was driving a stick shift.

"Um, no. You should stay. Have a nice time," I said without making eye contact—protocol.

"Wait! You can come over here and talk to me while I finish," he remarked.

"Nope. I didn't sign up for this. I'm out. Have a nice night," I said in a no-nonsense tone.

Second date? What do you think? Yeah, me too.

THL   THL   THL

Now, I don't expect you'll have dates this bad. You're smart enough not to encourage them and not to frequent the kinds of establishments I'm fond of. I'm okay with being the weirdo here. But I'd like you to notice that this was first date #98. I went on twenty-three more, and thankfully none of them were quite like this one, but it did take that many more before I met my partner.

A reporter recently asked me, "Why is it that some women have great success and get married from online dating, while other women have horror stories and terrible luck?"

"Easy!" I said. "The women who have great success and get married do so because they keep going."

You see, I have stories that could curl your mother's hair—and there are more to come—but I didn't let them stop me. Can you imagine if you stopped eating altogether after tasting something unpleasant? Stopped working out when you felt discomfort or got sore? Some women do, and I can see why—it can be hard going. But I'd do it all again—all 121 dates—just to get to him. It was worth it. And look at all the stories I have to tell!

Rookie Mistakes We Make

The most common and unfortunate rookie mistake women make might not be what you think it is.

We wait.

We wait to date. We have such logical reasons for waiting. We wait until we're "ready" and for the timing to be "right." It's the "I want to but . . ." thing we all do. Maybe you want to go online but it's almost the holidays or your birthday. Maybe you want to start but the timing will be better after you come back from that girls' vacation you have scheduled three months from now.

Maybe you're waiting because you're in school. Maybe you'll wait until after this one class, since it's kinda hard and the teacher is a real pain in the ass. Maybe you'll get back into dating when that's over. Or maybe you'll just wait until you're out of school. Or until after you have that master's degree . . .

Maybe you're fully employed, but you're going to wait until your work slows down, since it's insanely busy right now. You're not even able to keep up with your email (most of us can't, by the way). Or maybe you're waiting for that time-consuming work project to come to a close.

Sister, I hate to break it to you, but life doesn't get less busy. There will always be something else occupying your time, and people will always need things from you.

Here's a "good" excuse that lots of us have given ourselves at one point or another: You're waiting because you want to lose that extra poundage. Maybe it's five, maybe it's fifty, but you're going to wait until the weight is off. If I'd waited to lose the weight (mine was the fifty), I would have gone on exactly zero dates. I've forever and always wished to lose an extra couple of dozen pounds. You might think you need to drop down to a competitive "single" weight so you can land the right mate, because you're certain the best person for you—the best possible one you can get—will only like you at your "ideal" weight, not the one you're at right now.

I'm just gonna tell it like it is: You might never lose the weight. Then again, you could. And when you do—right when you're a few pounds away from that ideal weight, you'll go on a dating site, and do you know what'll happen? You'll meet your beloved. It will be amazing. And you'll be thinking, "Wow, he's *really* going to like me more once I hit that ideal weight. I'm so close." But do you know what happens next? The wooing begins. Yep, you're courting. The two of you go out for fancy dinners and midnight milkshakes, and before you know it your inner critic is screaming at you, telling you he only liked you in the first place because you almost made it to your ideal weight, and now that you're putting on five pounds (or so) he won't like you anymore and it will be over. That little voice in your cranium is telling you you're blowing it with the best one ever.

Don't listen to the critic. Date now, just as you are. And if you feel like you want to lose weight, fantastic; you can do that. And when you meet him, you'll be the size you are now or potentially slightly smaller. If you lose some weight while you're together, excellent; you wanted that. If you accidentally gain a few pounds back during the wooing, it's no problem, because you can remind your inner critic that he already picked you, as you were, at the higher weight. It's not a bad idea to date now instead of waiting—you already know he likes you as you are, and if you gain or lose a little, you have wiggle room.

A note to the big girls: If someone tells you that in order to fall in love you need to be skinny, run. Run as fast as you can in the opposite direction. Possibly toss a drink in their face and then run. If you're a big woman, you rock it. You will have dates; I did.

The reality is that the majority of men on mainstream sites are looking for thin or average body types. Our thin sisters have us beat here, but they aren't getting quality dates all day long, either. My hot, super-fit, sexy sister Sara says that once she got to her ideal body weight and fitness, the men started swarming . . . and they all want to sleep with her and comment on her body parts. Yuck! So it's no better on the other side. Sorry, my friends, there's no winning this body-image game. I suggest loving where you live and telling the game to stick it.

I was deflated when I first surfed around online trying to find a good dating expert or matchmaker and other dating services. Their websites are flawless, featuring the glamorous and perfect. The professionals and their clients were pretty, but all I could think was: *So what are you going to do for me? I'm a curvaceous (size 16) middle-aged woman looking for love, not a candidate to be the next top model in a Kate Spade ad.*

Thankfully, we all have bodies, and there's someone out there admiring yours just as it is. Just as we come in different shapes and sizes, people's preferences range from different shapes and sizes. I spent five years of my life researching men and their "type," and by the end of all that research what I found is that we women are much more critical of ourselves than men are. Men have a type or several types (just like you do), and for some men their type has nothing to do with body shape. It has to do with intellect or hair length or the way you move or the way you sound—or something else entirely. So don't discount your own shape thinking it's not hot, because it is.

We've learned that if you're fit, you get more attention. Not necessarily positive, loving, quality attention, but more attention. If you're big (like me), you'll get results, even if they aren't quite as immediate. You need to be willing to show yourself. Show that you're smart, funny, sexy, and sane. And for the love of all that's holy, show your body; don't hide it! Again, rock what you have!

Another reason you might be waiting to date is that you might be waiting to be in the mood. This was a big one for me. Turns out I was never in the mood before I got started. I'm guessing you might not be in the mood, either. Just like you're most likely not in the mood to get on the treadmill, but about fifteen to twenty minutes in, you're happy to be there. Dating can be like that. I'm always happy to have worked out, but I'm never in the mood to do it beforehand. Don't wait to be in the mood. The time to date is right now. Not next month, not next season—now.

When you wait for the right time to date, a whole lot of time can slip by without your ever really noticing. If you enjoy being single, that's fine—no problem. But if your goal is to be partnered, you're burning daylight in your life. Take a look through your calendar and count the last five dates you've had with five different people. How much time has passed? If it's more than three months since you've had all five, consider the possibility that you may not actually be looking for a partner. You might say you're looking for your partner but you're not taking actions to make it happen. Don't beat yourself up; change your routine instead, and start seeing people with more regularity.

Another big one is buying into the myth that "there are no good men out there." How often do you hear, "There just aren't any satisfactory single, straight men out there!" or "They're either gay, married, or don't have a job"? I could rattle off a dozen more such statements, but guess what: not one of them is true. There's no shortage of "good" men out there. This scarcity mentality dominating our culture and scaring women into thinking it's nigh impossible to find a good partner is crap. With more than seven billion of us on the planet, there's no shortage of people, and I believe we're still sitting at 50 percent men and 50 percent women (give or take).

Another doozy of a reason to wait to start dating: encouraging a long courtship before a first date. Have you been here? I definitely have. Let me set the scene: Take a bunch of time to get to know him before you meet in person. Deepen that relationship by allowing for a long prelude to your first date. Take two weeks to three months to learn about each other. Connect by talking on the phone so long your ear goes hot and you fall asleep together on the phone at bedtime. Write epic emails in short-story form. Text sexy messages all day. Flirt. Fill him in on your life story and the details from your day. This is a way to create real intimacy.

Excellent strategy?

No. Terrible strategy.

Do this, and when you meet for the first time at Chez Fancy for your long-awaited romantic dinner two months into your "relationship," you'll find out in two seconds that there's no physical attraction or chemistry for you (or for him or for both of you) and it's over. All that precious time wasted. All those hopes and dreams you pinned on each other will fall to the ground at the maître d' podium. Now, are you two ready to be seated to get this incredible date started?

"But . . . but what if . . . ," you might be thinking. I hear ya. Sometimes due to travel or children or your life schedule, you can't meet up quickly. I highly recommend meeting as soon as possible, however. I've found that, in general, waiting longer than ten days is too long. And if you're staying in touch while you're out of town on business, keep it light and don't invest a lot of yourself or your time. Give an upbeat response, letting him know you look forward to your date on your return. And if it does turn into that yummy, connected back-and-forth exchange, manage your expectations. This might sound harsh, but remember, this person may not be anything like you're imagining him to be.

Still not convinced? For your entertainment, allow me to present a date where I did exactly what I'm begging you not to do.

Date #26
Talk, Talk, Talk

Setting: Dinner at Fisherman's Wharf, San Francisco, CA

We lived more than two hours apart—not a great plan for a solid relationship. It took a while to meet in person, so we spent some quality time together via telephone.

I loved his voice, and I give good phone too. Night after night, we talked on the phone for hours. By the second week our schedules aligned and we made plans to meet. He picked the restaurant, promising something fancy with white linen tablecloths in a romantic setting in a neighborhood he loved.

Disclaimer: I'm going to sound like a snotty, judgmental bitch now. Are you ready?

He picked a tourist restaurant in San Francisco's Fisherman's Wharf—and not an old-world establishment, either. It was akin to a run-of-the-mill chain restaurant, and I'm being generous at that. It would have been a kind gesture on my part to pick the restaurant. I have twenty-three years of city dining and foodie experience, which went to waste in one moment. When we got there, he expressed his displeasure of his choice, while I tried to make the best of it.

So the restaurant wasn't what we'd hoped for. I wasn't what he'd hoped for, and he wasn't what I'd hoped for, either. We decided that since we both lived an hour away from the city and we'd commuted there to meet, we'd make the best of it. We ate, went to a club South of Market, and eventually said our good-byes.

Hot Tip Don't date someone who lives farther away than you're willing to drive three times a week. Don't get invested and bonded over the phone. It's not real—at least not the kind of real you're looking for. You need to see if there's tangible, live chemistry when you're face-to-face.

If he doesn't know the city or the restaurant scene as well as you do, then do both of you a favor by giving him two or three choices in different price ranges. Send him links to online reviews so he can be involved in the final choice.

5

Put On Your Dating Cap

I wasn't a dater. I was a serial monogamist. A cute guy and I would "hang out" until we were in a default-style relationship. Men found me (or I found them), one after another, and I did everything I could do to attract them right into a committed relationship—good, bad, inappropriate, or well-matched relationships alike. But there was never a clear evaluation to see if we'd make compatible long-term partners. I was interested in winning the prize and then evaluating the prize once I'd won it to see if I wanted to keep it, fix it, change it, or get rid of it. The truth isn't always pretty, and this is, for many women, a natural relationship pattern—a pattern I'm intimately familiar with.

When I first realized that I'd never really *dated*, I was almost forty. Excluding my ex-husband, the men I'd been "in a relationship" with would never have passed as compatible partners if I'd actually been looking at them through a dating process instead of my regular MO: "Oh, you're cute; you're in front of me. Yes, let's do this!"

When I realized that method wasn't working for me, I employed a revolutionary strategy called dating. I thought I might go on a dozen or so first dates and then I'd find him. I started dating by doing everything. I put up an online profile on the dating sites. I went to Meetup.com groups and other activities for singles. I started wearing makeup to the grocery store and made sure my yoga pants weren't too ratty. I told all my friends they could set me up on a blind date. I was ready.

Now What?

One of the fastest ways to attract someone . . . drumroll . . . is by attracting someone. In other words, do everything you can think of that you're comfortable with, and some things you're not so comfortable with but think you could push yourself to try, and anything else anyone else can help you think up: online dating, random chance meetings like seeing the guy who smiles at you every morning at Starbucks, or that guy your aunt's been trying to set you up with since college. Go for some test drives—preferably close together. Once you change your mind-set from "It'll happen one day" to "No reasonable offer refused," that's when things start to happen.

I know a woman who met her boyfriend on a plane. She flew all the time and had never met anyone that way before. He showed up only after she had tried everything else, including online dating. When you date and your numbers go up, you will attract more people from every avenue. It creates the buzz, and the Universe responds at a rapid rate.

Get on a Roll, Stay on a Roll

When I started dating, I went on twenty-four first dates in three months, and within that time, I went on several second and third ones too. It was a very busy summer. The first thing I discovered was that I didn't feel like dating at the start of the process. It took something to get myself motivated—to say yes to a man, clean myself up, and take myself out to meet him, when, honestly, there were reruns of *Law & Order* to watch and my dog is always up for snuggling. What I learned next—that this dating process could actually be *fun*—happened after about the fourth date. I was on a roll. It became enjoyable instead of painful. I looked forward to a night out with a new person instead of various shades of, "Is this guy going to be wasting my valuable time?" I was genuinely excited about who I got to meet that day.

Then I stopped. And guess what? Just like riding a horse or a bike, when I got out of the saddle for a while, even a couple of weeks, it was hard to get back on, but I never really forgot how. Remember to pace yourself, and don't beat yourself up if it takes a while to get back into the groove.

It's a Numbers Game

It's all about quantity to find your quality. If you're ready to date and you're truly looking for your mate, I recommend shooting for one to two dates a week.

If you want to find your best match and don't like dating, I'm sorry for the bad news, but brace yourself for this: from what I've seen, you need to be willing to have one-on-one time with between thirty and one hundred (yes, one hundred!) people to have a chance of meeting someone who's right for you. Now, does this mean you have to go on this many dates? Not necessarily, but you have to be willing.

I tell this to every single woman who will listen. A friend of mine would cringe every time she heard me say it. She told me, "Wendy, I'm just not willing. Even thirty different dates sounds like too many to me." She jumped into a long-distance relationship with the first handsome, charming guy who paid attention to her, and they were wildly mismatched. She didn't get what she needed from him, and ultimately he broke her heart. The second guy she was interested in lived exactly halfway around the world, and they started a Skype relationship. They were engaged to be married before they'd ever met face-to-face. She sold all her belongings to move to be with him. She ended up giving up her livelihood, her friends, and her home to start her new life, and now she's back in Seattle and at square one—all within a year's time.

My friend wasn't willing to risk being uncomfortable during the sorting process. Instead, she relied on magical thinking, hummed a few bars of "Someday My Prince Will Come," and hoped for her fairy-tale happily-ever-after. She's not alone; most of us have done some version of this (including me). Sometimes it does end up working out, but for the rest of us, it's high time we ditch the *Cinderella* narrative and start practicing what works—not what we *hope* will work. In my experience, one out of every ten dates has potential. Hang in there, take care of yourself along the way, and remember that (for some of us) somewhere around thirty dates might be just the beginning—so cut yourself some slack.

To Pursue or Not to Pursue (That Is the Question)

I would like to believe that a man who likes you will pursue you. Many men say they'll move mountains, jump through hoops, and do whatever it takes to find out who that woman is and how to contact her. Some guys aren't quite that confident. I've heard men say that leaving their number is a tactic to get her to make the first move, but in general, most men like to pursue.

Usually men also need to have some assurance that when they do pursue, you'll say yes. You may have heard a man say he'd like a woman to initiate a date, that it would be refreshing if a woman approached him. He likes that kind of confidence. Well, there's a big difference between you approaching and you pursuing. You can be noticed by a man without asking for his number or asking him out directly.

When I dug deep into interviewing men on women pursuing, most men said they weren't as attracted if a woman asked him out or made the first move, even when he was initially attracted to her. This doesn't mean you can never make the first move; rather, I'd take it as a hint to tread lightly. I don't think it's the case for every man, especially older men, and it's certainly not the case for online dating. When you're on a website with millions of people, you may need to make the first move; otherwise he probably won't find you.

So what's the best approach? How do you avoid coming on too strong? You simply "drop the handkerchief." Ever watch film noir movies from the 1940s, where the female lead "accidentally" drops a handkerchief and the man runs up behind her to retrieve it and hands it back? See if he picks up what you drop. Send a short but friendly line of interest, and if he picks it up and runs with it, great. If he doesn't, keep moving as if you'd never written to him in the first place. We'll cover more this in the chapter on online dating, but before we move on, I'd like to address and respectfully disagree with some of the "experts" out there. There's a strategy floating around that goes something like this: Never make the first move. Never speak first. The one who speaks first loses all the power and will never have the upper hand in the relationship dynamic from there on out. This is crap. Anytime you hear someone say "never" or "always" when they're giving advice—especially where dating is concerned—I'd recommend being skeptical.

When I was twenty-two, I approached a man and spoke first. He turned out to be my loving, devoted, and adoring husband for twelve years, and although he's not my husband now, he's been my "family" and a significant person in my life since 1990. Needless to say, I'm happy I approached. Most of the best men I have dated were ones I contacted first. I'd hate for you to miss out on the time of your life or the man of your dreams because you hoped he would approach you first. And for the record, I wouldn't be in my beloved partnership with Dave (#121) if I hadn't made the first move. (He did make the rest of them, though.)

My next dating story is an example of what "dropping the handkerchief" might look like. I was obvious, but my strategy (as much as you could call it a strategy) was effective.

Date #5
How to Be a
Successful Groupie 101

Setting: Drinks at Murphy's Irish Pub, Sonoma, CA

In true small-town fashion, I'd met #5 about six months earlier while sitting at a long table with twelve friends at Murphy's Irish Pub. Murphy's is the congregating place for everyone Irish and English in town, of whom there are many. I was often the only American at the table. In a small alleyway just off historic Sonoma Plaza, Murphy's is home to many foreign beers and the best bread pudding I've ever had.

It was a hot summer day when I first laid eyes on this charming British man. He was funny, friendly, irreverent, and well educated. I asked around about him, and finally a friend said, "Oh yeah, I know who you're talking about. He's a musician. He's playing at Murphy's on Friday."

On Friday, while getting ready to go out, I neatly printed my name, email address, and phone number on a Post-it. I paper-clipped it to a crisp five-dollar bill and tucked it away in my billfold.

At intermission, the tip cup was passed around. I waited for that moment when the cup and the talented musician were reunited, but he hadn't started playing his next set.

I pulled out the fiver with the Post-it attached, took a deep breath, and strolled up to him.

"Hi there. We've met before. I think it was about six months ago," I said.

A line creased his forehead and he said nothing.

"We were all at one big table outside. I don't expect you to remember. We only got to talk for about fifteen minutes. Here's the thing. I think you're interesting. If you asked me out, I'd say yes. My contact information is on this Post-it." I shoved it into the tip bowl with the attached bill, smiled, and walked away.

So what happened?

We dated for a few months, and as things progressed we could both see that we were better as friends. He learned to play "Vincent Black Lightning," an incredibly difficult and fast song, just for me, and he performs it magnificently. Richard Thompson would be proud.

 The Post-it note worked. He loves to tell that story.

6

The Art of Flirting

I used to think flirting was all about batting eyelashes, flipping and twirling hair, or giggling at his jokes. I once saw a woman cram her index finger into her mouth, twist it, and pull it out slowly while licking it. I was never willing to do any of these things, and while stuff like this—from the tame to the decidedly not-so-tame—might work for some, it's best to explore your own genuine style.

I'm terrible at flirting with strangers. I mostly take a direct approach just short of a proposition. How to flirt is not a mystery: simply make eye contact and smile. It's simple, all right, but not always easy. Since this is my weak spot, I enlisted the help of a friend who is a real pro. My dear friend McKenna has the art of flirting down. She knows how to work a room like no one's business. While watching her flirt, I was amazed and impressed yet felt somewhat deflated because her flirting was, in a word, flawless.

Since McKenna was born into her family business, one that requires charm and networking skills, I assumed that she had gotten an early start on learning to flirt. She can walk into any room and stand tall and confident with her million-dollar smile. She winks and laughs, and with her bright, sparkly eyes, she can systematically make every man in the room think he is the most special person there, regardless of the other dozen or so men circled around her, all vying for her attention. She's brilliant.

After sharing my perspective, McKenna said, "Wendy, no! You make flirting sound so inaccessible, like you have to be beautiful or have something like a special superpower to do it. Everyone can do it. It really is simple and effective—not just for me but for anyone who tries to do what I do."

I asked McKenna to break it down for us mere mortals, and here's what she said: "To me, flirting is engagement and fun; it's playful. It's not done with seriousness. It doesn't have to be sexual. I am ultra-selective and discriminating sexually, so flirting is a way to engage with a man to find out if I want to get to know him more. I keep my sexuality out of it. I play amorously with my eyes in conversation to encourage him. It's subtle; I don't bat my eyelashes."

Here's How I Flirt

As always, your mileage may vary, but here's a little something to get you started if flirting doesn't feel all that natural to you. Start with eye contact. A man will pick up on eye contact but sometimes won't know if it's intended for him, so once your eyes meet, hold his gaze and look away slowly with a shy smile. I wait a second or two and glance back with another small smile so he knows it's for him.

A man once told me, "A smile is the lubrication of life." Not a pageant-y toothy grin—that's trying too hard. A relaxed, authentic, lasting smile simply because you want to smile. After you make eye contact and send the smile, you have to be in a place where he can come over to you if he's interested.

A note about the girl pack: standing in the middle of a group of friends doesn't invite him to come over. If you're out on the town with the girls, stand apart from the pack or, better yet, find a way to break away from it a bit so he can approach you. Guys don't want to be rejected in front of all your friends. If you stand on the outside of your circle, it gives him a chance to walk past you and possibly say hello or gauge your level of interest and approachability. If you just want to hang with your girls, then stick together; most men won't even attempt to breach the circle. Try walking to the restroom alone; you just might bump into each other on your way back to your friends, or once back you can position yourself in a place where he can approach you safely.

Try breaking away to stand next to him while he's in line for a beer. He may start a conversation or offer to buy you a drink.

One time I saw a cute guy at the airport having his shoes shined. So I—someone who has never had her shoes shined—sat down next to him for a shine. If I had just walked by, we would not have met. He looked up, I said hi with a smile, and he did the rest. We dated for three months.

When I flirt, I laugh and make simple, sweet, teasing jokes because I love humor. It's easy for me and it keeps things light, fun, and interesting—at least for me. Sure, my flirting doesn't work with every man, nor should it. It comes from me, and it naturally weeds out those not interested in my type. It's much easier to date those who like my personality than those I feel the need to impress. Men will either select themselves into my conversation or out. Either way, it's a good thing because all I have to do is be myself. I don't take it personally if he doesn't ask for my phone number. I enjoy the adventure of it. If you can bring yourself to the mental and emotional place where the adventure itself is just as enjoyable as the potential outcome, then you're golden.

Sometimes, even if you're enjoying yourself, there's no zing. No butterflies. If a flirtation starts and you're not feeling it, a man will understand there's no spark. Let him down honestly and easily. He will respect and appreciate you for it. (Thanks for that, McKenna!)

Men usually know what to do with a sexually adventurous woman, but they don't know what to do with a nonsexual flirt. A nonsexual flirt is an anomaly and men don't usually have any experience with this dating "unicorn." Our culture promotes sexuality in everything and that's what men are used to; this can make flirting scary. Some men haven't had anyone show interest in them in a while, and if they are perceiving sexual advances from your flirting, they may think it means more than you intend. Don't panic; you can stop the conversation at any point for any reason. Just because you flirt doesn't mean you're obliged to do anything with anyone. You're the gatekeeper, so it's okay to flirt as long as you can set your boundaries.

If he says things like, "I bet you'd be hot in bed," or "Damn, what I'd love to do to you," change the subject. Or try this, in your kindest voice (the voice you would use if he wasn't misbehaving), say "I'm sorry, I think you misinterpreted this conversation," or "I'm sorry, I think you misinterpreted my intent. I thought we were chatting to see if we had something in common." Now pause, this is his cue. See where he leads you from there. He will tell you everything you need to know if you want to keep dancing, metaphorically speaking. If you're not looking for heavy sexuality in flirtatious interactions, don't encourage it. If you are, then enjoy.

Most men are looking for someone to return their attention, for eye contact, and for engagement in conversation. This is the simplest form of flirting: just listen, hold eye contact, and laugh when it's appropriate.

As I said, my flavor of flirting is direct. I smile and toss out one (hopefully clever) line and wait to see how it lands. I'm a much better "closer" when I'm on a date versus flirting with a total stranger. And even though flirting is my weakness, when I was single I still tried—a lot.

I used to worry about being too flirtatious, and tried to monitor the level of my flirting. A friend once said, "It's not your business to worry about that. Your job is to flirt." Men will let you know when to stop and when to continue if you pay attention to how things are feeling between the two of you as you interact with each other.

Use every opportunity to hone your social skills. When you're out in the world, talk to strangers and even flirt with them. Doing this may help you get a date. And if nothing else, it'll make you more comfortable with flirting when you're on a date. You'll find your style if you're willing to try. Practice makes (somewhere near) perfect.

7

Where Are All the Single Ones?

Tell me again, where are all the single, eligible people?

One of my clients, a gorgeous, petite, blond, blue-eyed woman in her midthirties, said, "I just can't seem to find men." By her looks, I knew she wouldn't have a problem attracting men. I began the interrogation.

"What are the qualities you'd like in your mate?"

"Well . . . ," she started, "I'd like him to be at least a little success-ful in business, but he doesn't have to be rich or anything."

"Okay. What else?" I asked.

"Oh, I want him to be well traveled, or at least he has to like to travel." She rambled off several other characteristics, none of which seemed unreasonable.

My next question: "Where do you work? Do you think you could meet men through your company or through companies that work with your company?" Since it's where 20 percent of couples meet, it was an obvious question.

She could hardly bring herself to meet my eyes when she muttered, "I'm a flight attendant for United Airlines in the first-class section for international flights." Um . . . hello. I don't know where else I could find a captive audience of men that would be more prequalified than international first class. I know more than one married woman who met her husband while slinging drinks in the sky.

Silvia, a software developer in her late forties, once said to me, "No one ever looks at me. I swear I am looking and no man looks back." She's insistent, thinks she's right, and feels utterly alone.

"You mean, no qualified men look at you," I reply.

See, we get checked out all the time. Truly, we do. We think we have our eyes open, but we don't. Test it: go out with your best girlfriend and walk a mall or a park and give her permission to smack your arm every time you miss someone checking you out. You'll feel the repeated sting from the thwacking as she points out person after person giving you a once-over. I don't care if you're twenty-two, forty-four, or sixty-five—we get checked out, and you're a particular flavor of adorable that appeals to more people than you think!

The problem is you aren't watching. Be present, look around, and smile. We think "no one looks at me" because we refuse to look at a those who might be looking at us when we look less than ideal. You know how you dress when you're just running to Target? Those yoga pants might not even be clean when you put them on. You need a baseball cap because you haven't washed your hair in three days and you don't have any makeup on. You don't feel worthy of a suitor's attention so you purposely don't look to see who's looking and you hope no one does. You're sure no person of quality would desire you in this state, and if he did, you'd question his judgment. Am I right?

Hey, ponytail girl. Yep, you. Those oversized sunglasses don't come with invisibility power. He can see you, and many men report that the ponytail-yoga-pants-big-shades look is actually one of their favorites. I did some pedestrian research around this by asking my seven hundred–some Facebook friends to forward the question, "What do you think of women in yoga pants?" to the men they know.

The stories of appreciation, admiration, and awe poured in. Most of the workshops I lead have a panel of four men who answer women's questions for an hour. I have had more than one "man panel" speak enthusiastically about their great love of yoga pants for fifteen minutes straight. Now, does this mean you should never dress up again? It's sweatpants and muumuus from here on out? Of course not. But don't cheat yourself out of the opportunity to meet somebody just because you've decided you look less than ideal that day.

Here's another favorite question: "Where can I find single guys?" The question almost answers itself. Single people are either

1. Not where you're looking for them, or . . .
2. Right there! But you haven't looked up from your phone long enough to see them.

We've already talked about Group 2, so let's tackle Group 1. First tip? Go look somewhere else. Do something different or go somewhere new. I spent many, many hours working in cafés. I'd go to different cafés during different times and sit at community tables, which are increasing in popularity these days.

Do you like pilots? Go to the airport. (I'm serious!) Lawyers? Try lunch at the pub or nice restaurant across the street from the courthouse.

Walk your neighborhood. Do you walk your dog every morning? Do five more minutes of grooming before you leave the house (you, not the dog), and when you're out, actually look up and smile at the people who walk by. The extra primping isn't for them, by the way—it's for you, for your confidence. If you don't see anyone, change up your route or your walk times.

"I wouldn't date anyone who lives in my neighborhood," you say? Throw your furry pal and leash in the car and give yourself an upgrade. Drive to the nicer neighborhood up the hill, park, and walk there. Over the ten years I spent being single, my beloved dogs, Eloise and Lilly, walked in the nicest neighborhoods of Sonoma, Marin County, Oakland Hills, and San Francisco—we scouted them all.

Now, don't tell me that you don't have a pet so this won't work for you. I "researched" it, and it turns out walking alone is 100 percent acceptable behavior these days. Stroll. Comment on how amazing that landscape looks as you're passing by the homeowner who's out there pruning. You could ask, "Is that an olive tree?" or "Does that grow well in our climate?" For the urban dwellers, try, "Do you know how far it is to the river from here?" All you've gotta do is give him an opening.

Where else might you find your mate? At work. Yeah, I said it: your workplace. My friend Stephanie Losee, coauthor of *Office Mate: The Employee Handbook for Finding—and Managing—Romance on the Job*, says that roughly half of us will date someone at work at some point in our working lives.[4]

Of couples who date at work, 20 percent marry. If you date your boss or your subordinate, the likelihood that you will marry is roughly double: 44 percent. This higher percentage is due to it being a much higher risk; couples only accept the risk if they think there's something there, like true love. And think about it: during the job interview, aren't you picking each other because you can both tell there's compatibility, humor, strength, and the potential for a good partnership? Those things also make for a good foundation for a romantic relationship.[5]

Oh, you work from home, huh? Me too. How about trying your local farmers' market? Try looking around at the men near you and maybe make eye contact with a few instead of solely focusing on the ripeness of the loganberries.

Where do you shop? Grocery stores are the gatekeepers of the food that super-sexy people eat. Want a conversation starter? Ask about anything on the shelf in front of you, unless you're in the condom and lube aisle. (Wait a minute; let's not limit ourselves here. That aisle might be your signature pickup spot.) Use your favorite store as a resource for mate shopping.

Your local computer or gadget store on a Saturday morning is guaranteed to be jam-packed with people just waiting around for their appointment. Strike up a conversation about one of the newest gadgets.

Go to the nearest home improvement store and you'll be among those who probably own their home and like doing things with their hands. Ask one of them where you can find something, because you both know it can be tough to track down an employee.

At the gym men know that most women don't like to be hit on. They think it's because we think if they do, they're creepy. I'd say that for some women that might be true. But for others, we don't want attention because not only do we not look our best but we're also sweaty. Eww. How could he be attracted to that? I'll give you a hint. Where else can you find us covered in sweat with our hair a mess? Many men *still* won't make a move. He may think you're gorgeous but he doesn't want to be Creepy Gym Guy. Another missed opportunity, unless you step up and say, "Does that machine only work the shoulders or does it also work arms?"

Go to an open mic night at your favorite haunt and show off your talent. I have gotten myself invited to speak at storytelling events, on stage and in front of about a hundred people. When you're on stage, whether it's singing, comedy, storytelling, or participating in a skit (even karaoke works), your new friend (the one you haven't met yet) will have a chance to grasp your style, and after you've performed they can sort out putting themselves in front of you, if you bother to hang around the venue's public areas—not just the greenroom, rock star.

Normally, going to bars is the last place most of us looking for lasting relationships, but there are success stories. If I were going to attempt such a feat, I'd try a nice place in the financial district at 5:45 PM on a Friday. Why? It might be the only time that cute over-worked executive can be cajoled and pried away from his desk to go with the gang to celebrate the win from the week.

Don't be afraid to be creative. I once asked a man at a gas station, "Do you like your Audi A3? I've been eyeing them lately, wondering if they're sound cars."

Finally, date online. The same fine people you'll meet in real life are also online. All the cool kids (and cool not-kids) are doing it. If you think you're better than that, it's time to get over that particular hang-up. You're missing out. I love online dating because it's where men (and women) go *specifically* to find someone to date. That cute guy in the grocery aisle isn't necessarily looking for a date.

Amazing people are everywhere. And your best invitation is a direct look and a smile. If you feel you need to say something to catch his attention, say it. Drop the handkerchief. Give him an open-ing and see if he picks up what you're laying down. It's that simple.

Hot Tip The two of you are talking. You can tell he likes you back. The moment seems to be ending because you're both too shy or it's awkward. Say this: "I would say yes to you if you asked me (blank)." You fill in the blank: to coffee, on a date, to go to bed with you—however you want to finish that sentence is your business.

Sheepdogs

Challenge yourself to be receptive. For some of us, receptivity is dif-ficult because we think, whether from direct experience or instinct, that all men are scary or dangerous. Our society, our girlfriends, our parents, and even other men have told us that men are dangerous. We think of men like wolves in sheep's clothing, out to take what they can get. Sadly, this is sometimes true.

I know I'm going out on a limb here, but I want you to consider that most men are *not* dangerous. What if the men you're walking by on the street—the ones sitting across from you in cafés, reading the newspaper while they wait for their car to be washed, shopping at your neighborhood grocery store—what if these men were safe?

Before I go any further, I'm not telling you to stop paying attention to your own safety. I'm not telling you that because there are, undeniably, dangerous people in the world. Be alert. Listen to your gut. But at the same time, be open and willing to believe in the goodness of your fellow human beings.

The next time you're at your favorite restaurant, look around and do a quick head count. I bet that if something bad happened to you while you were dining, you would most likely have as many male personal heroes as there were men in your general vicinity. Again, this isn't to say you're not going to meet some real creeps—they're definitely out there—but most men will fall into protective positive roles rather than predatory ones when the opportunity arises. My girlfriend Ivory shared a date story where the evening just went sideways and she wasn't sure she was entirely safe. Because, like me, she believes that most men are our protectors and look for opportunities to be a hero, she flagged down a nearby stranger to help extract her from the situation, and her plan worked swimmingly.

Our culture widely promotes the concept that in the area of sex, sensuality, and the mere presence of female energy, men are a bunch of pigs who will consistently behave badly. But what if our culture is wrong? Maybe most men aren't pigs or wolves. Maybe most men are more like sheepdogs—fiercely protective, caring, and fun. Did you know that you can't tell the difference between a sheepdog and a wolf side by side if all you're looking at is their teeth? Maybe all we've ever seen is their teeth.

If you're interested in road-testing my theory, here's your job: as part of learning to be receptive to strangers while you're out in the world, pay attention to when and where men are looking out for you. Watch for when they come to your aid; watch where they have your back. You'll be surprised at what you find. Come join my world; it's a beautiful place.

Long-Distance Relationships

Long-distance relationships are rarely the real deal. Harsh statement, I know, but for many people, it's a way of avoiding being in a full-time relationship but still enjoying the status of saying, "I'm in a relationship."

If you're online dating and someone who lives far away from you is trying to date you, I suggest that you ditch the invitation. Write back the following:

"Thank you so much for your interest. I don't date outside my area. Good luck out there."

Define for yourself what "long distance" is for you, and do it now, before it becomes an issue. For me, I didn't date anyone I wasn't willing to drive to see three times a week. Your limit is your limit, whether it's two minutes, fifty miles, or four towns over.

When you start a long-distance relationship, even if you date for a long period of time, you won't know crucial details about your compatibility and a whole host of things about him until you've spent quality and quantity face time in close quarters together.

I had known a friend of mine for two and a half years. We talked nearly every day, from thirty minutes to hour upon hour. We weren't romantically compatible or even interested in each other, so we weren't on our best behaviors with each other; we were our authentic selves. We went on a fifteen-day trip together. We learned things about each other we had never known, and we learned how we worked things out as a duo. We also learned what didn't work in our friendship, and at the end of our trip, our intimate two-and-a-half year friendship was o-v-e-r. We never saw how ill-suited we were over the phone or during short weekend visits.

If you have a plan to convert a long-distance relationship to the real world, what I just said doesn't mean you need to break up with that sexy man you met in New York at your friend's Tribeca loft party. Even though you live in Palo Alto, I think you crazy kids should go for it. The times I've seen long-distance relationships work is when both people want to be together and they have an actual plan, with a city they will both be living in (together) by a particular date that isn't years away. Spend a considerable amount of time together 24/7. When one of you visits, stay at a vacation rental or a hotel; do not stay at that person's house, especially if the two of you don't know each other well.

Take an extended trip or two together. Trips are informative because they take you away from what you already know, out of your comfort zone, and you can see how you solve problems and make decisions together. Once all that has been accomplished, I'll green-light the relationship, my friend. Until then, though, tread carefully.

Date #21
Dear Chicago

Setting: Wedding weekend, Salt Lake City, UT

I took a trip to my hometown of Salt Lake City to attend the wedding of a dear friend. Of course, in good form, John had several pre-wedding festivities planned. The first drinking spot was Duffy's Tavern. As I slid into the large, round, eight-seat booth filled with old friends, a tall, handsome man appeared. I knew him. I'd met him sixteen years earlier when I was home (with my then husband) for a visit. Here we were all these years later, single, and he was looking at me.

Do you know what happens when you hook up with someone before a wedding? It means you have a date for the wedding. While this wasn't exactly our "first date," it was our first encounter in a romantic setting, and it went well for everyone. We had a total blast and were inseparable the entire extended weekend.

So what happened?

Chicago to San Francisco is an extraordinarily long commute. We traveled to see each other—my town, his town, out of town. Eventually we realized long distance wasn't what either of us wanted, but we still adore each other today.

8

Online Dating Sites: Where Your Date Looks When They're Looking for You

Are you ready to explore online dating? Let me tell you who you're going to meet out there: the same people you could meet out in the world. Seriously, the stigma of online dating is so 1990s.

The number one reason I advocate for online dating is this: statistics. It's the one place where the most single people go to meet other single people for a date. Period.

The number two reason I encourage you to date online is because you'll have access to those you don't normally have access to in your daily life. In my case, I work from home, and when I'm working in public, I'm leading workshops in conference rooms filled with women. The men I had access to in my day-to-day world were the checkers at my local grocery store and the postal package delivery driver. That's it. My partner, Dave, was running his company in an office park in Silicon Valley. We would have never met in a million years without OkCupid.

Online sites matched me with doctors, lawyers, and multi-millionaire public speakers. I met talented musicians, entrepreneurs, writers, executives of nonprofits, and just all-around great guys. Some men were connected with large and impressive circles of friends, yet they hadn't found their mate within those circles. I also met men who were recently single after having a long-term mate, and their all-too-familiar circle of friends didn't lend itself well to dating.

Men understand that online dating is the most efficient way to meet single women who want to date and get to know them, and men do what's easy and effective. Shouldn't we be looking to do the same?

Are there downsides to online dating? Sure there are. Sheena S. Iyengar of Columbia University and Mark R. Lepper of Stanford University conducted a study in 2000 that shows that if you put out twenty-four jams instead of six for people to sample at the supermarket, people will buy less jam. The presentation of too many jams leads some people to believe that somewhere out there in the world exists the perfect jam.[6] So many available daters on an online dating site can have the same downside: too many options.

Blogger Katherine Fritz shares this example:

When there are that many options, it's all the more frustrating that the obvious choice is harder to find. I would scroll through a seemingly endless supply of men who purportedly lived in my very own city but whom I had never seen before, until the only option was to just eliminate people for purely superficial reasons. Works in a bank? Boring. Has a cat? Eh. Has a beard? I guess I like beards. Went to Burning Man? Oh, dear, probably not. All the while, I was equally aware of how many of those same men had to be flipping through a seemingly endless supply of single women, staring at my profile and thinking, "Likes to read. They all say that. Mel Brooks movies? Whatever. Nice eyes, but a little pudgy around the middle."[7]

So yes, there are downsides to online dating, which is why many of us have a resistance to it. He says he wants to meet you and then he disappears. Or he connects, engages, writes for a while, and then disappears. This definitely happens, and I'm sorry if it happens to you. It leaves a girl feeling like she did it wrong. I am here to tell you that you *did not* do it wrong. If you're out there being yourself, you're doing it right. You couldn't have said it or done it differently to have it magically go well. Remember, the right partner comes back. The best mate for you follows up, initiates, and shows up for dates.

Sometimes he disappears because he sees you're not quite a match for him. Sometimes he disappears because he's new at online dating and he doesn't know what he's doing yet and it freaks him out. Sometimes he disappears because when you want to meet face-to-face and he isn't who he represented himself to be, he doesn't see another way out.

Repeat after me: "Him disappearing is about him, not about me."

And I'm sorry, I truly am. I'm sorry for every single time that happens to you. You're not alone—it's happening to hundreds if not thousands of your single sisters out there right now too.

All that said, it is worth doing. When I wasn't online dating, I wasn't dating much at all—and looking back, I am so glad I decided not only to try it out but to stick it out. So let's get started.

Which Online Site Is Right for You?

Including a referral list of online dating sites would be quaint but outdated five minutes after this book went to print, so instead I'm going to paint in broad strokes here.

Any entrepreneur can buy an off-the-shelf software suite that has every fancy button, wingding, bell, and whistle that the big guys like Match.com have and the interface can be customized for niche markets. Currently there's not a superior dating site based on technological features (unless you count OkCupid's fancy Q&A section).

How you pick your dating site is your decision alone. Match
.com has twenty-five million users and counting—plenty of singles
there. Are you looking for farmers only? (I'm serious; there's a site for
rural dwellers.) Jewish? People over fifty looking for people over fifty?
Partnershiplove.com is for transformational folks. Ivy League university graduates? There are specific sites for just about any single you can
think of. If you're looking for casual sex, that's available, and if you're
looking for kinky, BDSM-lifestyle people, yep, there's a site, or ten, for
you too. You name it, there's a site for it. Use Google; it is your friend.

Who do I like best? By the end of my dating experience, I appreciated Match.com and met wonderful men there, but I favored
OkCupid because I found the type of men I resonate with more often
on that site. But I'll speak to both sites.

Match.com still stays on the top of my faves list because it's the
ultimate mainstream site. You will see all kinds of people who want to
pay their Match.com membership to find a girlfriend or wife and leave
internet dating behind. Match.com is widely marketed, and their tele-
vision commercials are more and more frequent. Men often choose it
because it's the easiest route to take when they're focused on work and
only have a few moments to put into researching where they're going
to spend time enriching their personal lives.

I also like that they offer Match.com events—group singles' mix-
ers in larger cities.

One man said, "Match is like going swimming at the community
pool on the hottest day of the year. Everyone's there, including the
people you'd like to meet as well as tons of people you'd never want
to see in a bathing suit."

Yep.

I got a lot out of Match.com and met many amazing men.

My favorite: OkCupid. Why? Well, it's where I met Dave. It's also
where I met a number of men I liked quite a bit. For years I held a
grudge against the free sites. I was of the mind that if he couldn't

pay $35.95 each month to find true love, then he just wasn't committed. Why bother? Then, quite simply, I got over it. Why? Because bottom line, OkCupid is a cooler site with a fun, useful question feature. I wound up with more enjoyable men on more enjoyable dates through OkCupid, but it's all about flavor, so you'll need to find yours.

I first went on the OkCupid site after draining the Match.com pool. Yes, that really happened—I drained the Match.com swimming pool shortly after Date #70. My search parameters: I'm a woman looking for men, age forty-two to fifty-five within twenty-five miles from my San Francisco Bay Area home.

Match.com has a handy little button located at the top right of each man's photo that can be pushed. The button says, "Don't Show This Member Again." Once I make an assessment that a man is not my match, his "Don't Show" button gets pushed. This helps because I don't keep seeing the same not-my-man over and over again.

Sisters, by Date #70, I had pushed that button exactly 5,270 times. That's right: I'd looked at 5,270 men, all of whom may be wonderful but were not my man.

Here's the bigger issue: Guess how many remained in my search criteria? None. Zip. Zero. I was out. I'd seen them all. I'd been there. I'd tapped that and tapped out. That was when I shifted focus to OkCupid and jumped into a new pool.

When I signed up for OkCupid, setting up a profile was relatively easy except that they had this extra layer that seemed, well, a bit of a pain in the ass, honestly. I didn't understand the additional feature— the ability to answer questions and enhance (or detract from) your compatibility thanks to the answers to your questions.

But once I started answering these optional questions, I was hooked. I answered around 360 questions, which is average. Here are two sample questions:

"Do you love camping?" (I think this is a good question, since I don't camp.)

"Would you be concerned if your partner still masturbated, even though you were sexually active together?" (I think this is the dumbest question on there.)

See? Fun. Each seemingly little question ends up helping to paint the big picture that becomes your profile and closer matches you to the potential dates.

I went off the dating market before I got to use them, but I'm a big fan of new sites such as HowAboutWe, where you can say what you want to do and people bid for your time. For example, you can go to events you're dying to go to and you have the added bonus of a date. Now, that's smart dating. I also like these companies because they have you meet up with people right away, which I think is efficient and smart.

If you're using HowAboutWe to meet people to do things you already love (like playing tennis or going to a concert), then you have a quick start with a new person doing an activity that makes you happy and a date with very little pressure.

The apps that connect people instantly (like Tinder) get a bad rap for being too superficial, but I want you to consider the possibility that they can work to your advantage. They seem to get the ball rolling more easily and more quickly, with more people more often. There's no access to prejudging them for being a boring banker or for taking a past vacation at Burning Man.

My least favorite site is eHarmony. When I used the site it had a high monthly price tag and the system made me jump through all kinds of hoops to communicate with men. They created layers of contact that were useless to me when determining if I resonated with a person. I'm all about efficiency; I don't like wasting my valuable time on what someone's favorite color might be.

If you join, you fill out a time-consuming questionnaire (plan on taking an hour) and you can only see the matches that are sent to you. After taking the test, people who are only interested in casual dating are allegedly turned away. I have heard from more than one friend that they spent the time filling out the form and received a "We don't have any matches for you" response. Ouch.

Whichever site you choose, people will be looking for you. So let's look at online sites from a man's perspective, since men search, browse, and read profiles very differently than women do. A man browses a woman's profile by looking first at the main photo, just like you do. Your main photo is the most influential piece of your profile. (You evaluate everyone on their main photo too.) If he likes the first photo, he'll look at the rest of your photos. If he likes what he sees, he'll dig deeper into your profile. Your profile photo can make or break his interest and attraction for you. Make it a good one. You—natural smile, beautiful, happy, relaxed, easy you. I once heard a strategy: "Let him know what he's getting. Don't wear makeup; look like you do when you first wake up." My two cents: Sure, you *can* do that. It would be authentic, but Anthropologie doesn't throw a wrinkled sweater on a wire hanger and stick it in any random place in the front window. Your beauty is art. Don't stick a 99-cent frame around your masterpiece.

Now that we've uncovered the basics of online dating, let's start digging deeper into the fun stuff. To start, I'm not nearly done with photos. Read on, daters.

9

My Secret Tips for Online Photos

Yes, this merits its own chapter. You bet your booty it does. Your photos tell as much (if not more) of a story as your blurbs and any other information on your profile, so choose them wisely and take your time.

Your Primary Photo

This is your first impression, and first impressions matter. Ask a friend or an amateur photographer to shoot an amazing shot or ten of you and pick one of them as your primary photo. If you choose to pay a photographer, I recommend you hire one who specializes in "social" shots (that's code for online dating profile photos) because you've hired them to play the starring role as your best friend for the day. They'll shoot you in cafés, in the woods on a hike, in a park, by the ocean (hell, *in* the ocean if you want)—wherever you most wish to be seen.

Many dating experts advise you to have professional shots taken. I don't recommend the traditional style of professional studio shots. People have well-tuned bullshit meters. They're perceptive, and they know what airbrushing looks like; they've been looking at it in magazines and catalogs since puberty. When it's obvious that you've taken the route of pro shots, they're going to wonder what the real you looks like.

Simply shoot for natural, beautiful, relaxed, and happy, with no airbrushing or other digital retouching.

More Photos

Most online dating sites let you put lots of photos online. I recommend posting a minimum of three photos, including your primary shot. The best scenario is to use all-natural candid shots where you're the only person in the photo. Most if not all your photos should appear to be unstaged. As with your primary shot, you want to look current, sexy, happy, and natural.

Superficial or Super-Perceptive?

Most of us are visually oriented, but what are daters looking for in your photo? The same thing you're looking for: attraction. They'll look at your face, your hair, and your body. And if they're perceptive, they'll look beyond that to see what other clues they can glean.

- Do you take pride in your appearance?
- What's your style like?
- Do you seem like a happy person?
- Do you look stressed out?
- Do you look comfortable in your own skin?
- Do you seem high maintenance?
- Are you a type A or B?
- Are you surrounded by nine cats/parakeets/boa constrictors?
- Wait . . . *how* many children are in the shot?

Current. As In. The Last Twelve Months.

I know that adorable photo of you is only five years old. You swear you look the same today. Trust me, my friend, you don't. None of us do. Update your photos. Everyone's smartphone is equipped to do this, and with self-timers and self-timing apps readily available, you don't even need another person. You have no more excuses. Update!

Case in point: I once said yes to a date who wanted to try out the new dinner spot in town, but I scheduled coffee instead, as I assumed the young person in the photos on his profile would not resemble the twenty-year-older version I would meet that day. My hunch was accurate.

Children

Daters will always assume those seven adorable nieces and nephews in the shot are your biological children. Where profile-surfing is concerned, photos come first; reading comes last.

I recommend you not put any photos of children (yours or anyone else's) online. It's a public place, and you probably don't have their permission and true consent. It's a privacy thing, plain and simple.

Hobbies and Passions

Are you a runner? If five out of seven shots are of you running, the non-runners may pass you by (online—not on the track). If you're only trying to attract runners, you're doing a fine job of sorting. If you're trying to show you're athletic, one shot will do the trick. Pick the one of you doing a glory dance as you cross that finish line.

Business Photos

Do you have photos of yourself online anywhere else? Perhaps business photos? If you own your own company and there's a photo of you on the bio page of your website or if you're listed on any website at all—corporate, association, porn, whatever—and you use that headshot on your dating site, anyone can find out who you are and everything associated with you on that other website. What? Wait . . . how is this possible?

Google. Try it out for yourself. Go online. Open two browser windows. Be sure the second one's page is set to Google, like you're going to do a search.

Using the first search window, find a photograph of a person, say on a dating website. Click and drag the photo off the website page and drop it into the search bar of the second browser window and tab on over to Google Images. Voilà! Google finds that image anywhere and everywhere it lives online and spits out all kinds of associated information on that person.

Say you're a dating expert who's writing a book on your experiences on 121 first dates. Good idea to not use the photo of said dating expert from 121FirstDates.com (my website), yes? Yep, I learned this lesson the hard way.

Party Girl

If you're twenty-one and newly hitting the party scene, party on. If you're older, photos of you at parties, vacationing, and clubbing may not be interpreted the way you'd intended them to be. Photos of you boozing it up with a group may seem festive to you, but they also might make you look like the drunk girl or a potential hot mess. Anything you feature in your photos will be interpreted as a priority for you. Unless you are, in fact, an alcoholic and you're looking for someone to be cool with that, don't feature yourself getting your drink on in a party setting in all your photos.

One of you holding a glass of wine or champagne at a formal event (or the like) is just fine.

You with Family Members

Daters doesn't know you. They don't know your family. If you're standing with your brother, people are probably going to assume you're with your ex-boyfriend. Adding people to your photo just gives viewers a puzzle to solve without any information to go on. The focus shifts away from you and toward figuring out the scenario. Keep the focus on you.

You with Your Girlfriends

Men I've interviewed say they hate group photos. They have to struggle to know which one is you, and if your friend is hotter, they wonder where they can find her—and you're no longer as interesting. Do you want your date looking at other women? Do you want him comparing you to those other women?

Seattle Nate said, "Here's the thing: I can't help but compare everything. So when she shows me photos of her with her friend(s), it's automatic. I'm telling you, almost 100 percent of the time, her friends are cuter than she is. It cracks me up. Women need to find themselves uglier friends if they're going to be giving me group shots."

You with Other Men

Don't post photos of yourself with other men. It's amazing that I even need to address it, yet I see both men and women guilty of posting images of themselves with the opposite sex all the time. This includes the super-cute photo of you after a mediocre hack job of cutting him out.

You with Blurred or Cut-Out People

I don't care how good you look in that photo. Please don't use any photo that requires blurring or chopping; there are always remaining body parts and it just looks weird and mysterious—but not in an I-want-to-get-to-know-you kind of way.

Self-Portraits

Selfies are terrific if you can take one well. I couldn't; I was lousy at it. A selfie done well can make the viewer feel like they're making eye contact with you right now, which feels spontaneous and intriguing.

In the olden days, a selfie had bad lighting, cut off part of your body (usually your face), and was unflattering, uninformative, and uninteresting. But nowadays, with our phones and computers at our fingertips, it should be a snap (ha). Yay for technology!

What's the Difference between Sexy and Trampy?

Everyone is different with a different standard for sexy and trampy. This is helpful to keep in mind for photos and is also useful for dates. I interviewed several dozen men on this topic and here's what I learned: I assumed the respectable guy wants you in a turtleneck and the player wants you in a tube top. Surprisingly, I've met the opposite in both directions. It's all a matter of style.

Newsflash: Cleavage is in. It's completely acceptable, but ultimately you should wear your cleavage line where you normally would and where you're most comfortable. I'm a cleavage-y girl. I like it. I wear cleavage-revealing tops all the time. It's just how I roll, and that's how I represented myself in my photos. You should dress as you would if no one else were paying attention. Okay, maybe put a bra on if you think you need one, and keep those nipples tucked away. Captain Obvious here, but you never know.

Too much makeup versus not enough makeup: Again, it's a preference. Men are all over the map on this. Seattle Nate would like all women to wear a lot of makeup and know how to wear it well. Date #101 was happy to see me without any at all. It's a matter of taste.

I've researched what men thought "dressing slutty" meant. The men in this survey ranged from thirty-five to fifty-five. As always, what the men had to say did not disappoint. The majority of men said what's "too much" is when a woman is showing multiple body parts—and a lot of each. In other words, wearing an overly revealing top with a super-short skirt is too much. Take that top and pair it with a regular skirt or pants and you're fine. Or take that skirt and wear it with a less revealing top—also good. There; now we know.

Hot Tip A photographer friend once told me, "When you're taking your sexy shot, think, 'I know a secret.' It will give you a sweet, sexy, playful expression." Ever heard of the Mona Lisa smile? That's what you're going for.

Take the Feedback

Having your dates tell you, "You look so much better in person," is nice for you in the moment but it is not stellar news for your profile. Listen to their feedback. Reconsider your photos; think of all those other terrific, qualified matches you're missing because you're not accurately representing yourself.

If you're not receiving responses to your primary photo, mix things up. Move one of your other photos into primary position and see who you might attract.

Full-Body Shot

Always—and I mean always—put a full-body shot on your profile. Not an art shot. "What's an art shot," you ask? An art shot is where you have painstakingly positioned yourself in a way that strategically emphasizes your legs crossed in front of your body to hide your tummy. Or an art shot is where you've wedged yourself in a chair just right so that it cuts off half your butt in the shot. You can put that art shot on too, but that's not a "full-body" shot. And it's false advertising. You know it and I know it. If you can take a full-body self-portrait, they'll see you're not tricking them with a pro shot, or trying to hide where your curves begin and end.

Your body shot needs to show your whole body, and it should show your shape. Wear something that form-fits to your silhouette versus a baggy sweater and long skirt. This cuts down on first-date meet-and-greet disappointment, which is a total drag.

I know the importance of an accurate body shot, especially since I'm on the larger side. As I was asking around for help, an old boyfriend offered by saying, "I love your body. Can I take photos for you? I can shoot you in the right angles to highlight your assets."

Um, yes. He knew my body, he liked my body, and he knew what men like him would like about my body—it was a brilliant idea, and the photos came out well. I looked sweet and sexy, which is what he naturally pulled out of me when we spent time together. If you're friends with an ex, and it wouldn't be awkward or upsetting to him if you asked, let him take your photos. When you do, you'll have a sparkle in your eye (in the photos) since you sincerely appreciate and have an affinity for your photographer.

Not convinced that you need to put a body shot up? The next date emphasizes what can happen when you leave the most important photo out of your collection.

Date #9
Size Matters

Setting: Dinner at The Girl & The Fig, Sonoma, CA

Fingers tapping on my steering wheel, I was pressed for time, nervous, and hunting for the impossible: an available parking spot on the historic Sonoma Plaza at rush hour.

We'd had a prescreening phone call before making this dinner date. The topic revolved around size. He expressed his displeasure with how big he was, how he doesn't want to be big, and how he doesn't want to date big girls. Size dominated, so I wanted to be sure he had fair warning about my size. "I'm curvy," I said. "I'm not the skinny girl. I'm not quite plus-sized, but I am on the upper end of the spectrum. If you know anything about women's clothing size, I'm between a fourteen and a sixteen, which is not small—more like extra large." He assured me this was no problem.

I paused ten feet from the front of The Girl & The Fig bistro, since I could see that my date and I were arriving at the same time. As I paced my step as I walked toward him, he looked at me. He slowly scanned my whole package, from my freshly straightened medium-long brown hair down to my black sling-back, four-inch heels and eventually brought his head for a long and lingering gander all the way up again, until he met me eye to eye. His frown held tight while his head cocked slightly to one side. Even though he clearly thought he was fine with curvy girls, it was obvious that he hadn't been entirely honest with himself, or with me. I felt like I'd been kicked in the oversized gut.

Date #9 was looking for long and lean and got a curvy girl instead. Fuck. He opened the door for me and waited. This is where I blew it. This is where I should have said, "Thanks for driving all the way over here. Clearly, I'm not your girl, so let's not waste each other's time. We're skipping dinner. Have a nice evening."

Did I do this? Of course not. I could feel his impatience, and I didn't want to be impolite. I felt the pressure to not be displeasing so I walked through the restaurant door. We were seated in Morgan's section. Morgan's my favorite server at the Fig. Our table was situated on the gorgeous ivy-covered patio right next to the fireplace. This was my consolation. After a quick assessment of the situation, Morgan was giddy, his perma-grin directed at me. I'd been at this very table with another date two nights earlier. Morgan reveled in having fun at my expense.

"You're David, right?" Morgan asked my date.

"No."

"I swear I've seen you before. Are you a regular? Were you here two nights ago?" Morgan asked.

"No, I've never been here before," Date #9 said, agitated.

Morgan smiled, pleased with himself. He kept my anonymity by pretending he didn't know me as he slid inside jokes my way, poked at my date periodically, and winked at me.

I ordered a salad and assumed we'd whip through this quickly. My date did not oblige. He ordered an appetizer, a main course, a side dish after that, and dessert. It was a slow-w-w-w-w process. To make matters worse, he made no attempt to hide his annoyance that I was less than what he desired, and he took it out on me by not generating any of the conversation. I had to do all the heavy lifting. At one point, I stopped, sat back, and didn't say anything, hoping that would cause him to eat faster. It didn't. Ugh.

By the conclusion of the date, I ran to my car and called another man who had also been vying for that same Saturday night.

"Are you still free to meet tonight?"

"Yes. Come to the W Hotel restaurant."

Excellent. I drove myself the fifty miles into San Francisco as fast as I could, and when I arrived, my date looked me up and down from the top of my medium-long brown hair down to my black sling-back, four-inch heels, and met my gaze with his sparkling eyes, an enormous grin, and a long, warm hug.

One man's disappointment is another man's delight.

To save your spirit and prevent pain and frustration all around, it's important to put full-body photos on your online profile page, not just head shots and not an art shot that cuts off what you consider your unflattering part(s). It may seem superficial, but hey, physical attraction plays a major role for most people—both male and female—when choosing a potential mate. I'd expect the same from the profiles of the men I looked at online.

After the abysmal Date #9, I put accurate body shots online to let men sort me out before we met. I had this experience only one other time after Date #9. Not bad for 121 first dates.

If you're not feeling it or if he's not feeling it, leave. Don't waste another precious minute. You can end the date before it begins. You officially have my blessing. If you're stuck doing all the heavy lifting in a conversation, simply stop. Lean back in your chair and stop talking. This action will either elicit participation or effectively end the date. Either outcome is better than the torture you've already endured.

One way to pick yourself up after negative feedback or rejection is to get right back out there, putting yourself in front of another date to receive a positive "look." It might work, it might not, but I would have gone place to place that night just to balance the scales. Just like you, I'm a flavor. I'm not everybody's, but I'm definitely somebody's.

Date #10
My Hero

Setting: Drinks at XYZ Bar at the W Hotel, San Francisco, CA

Frazzled, late, rained-on, and ego-bruised from Date #9, I pushed my way through the dark, overcrowded XYZ Bar at the W San Francisco Hotel. I'm an old white lady in a sea of hip, young, racially diverse nightclub-goers. I'm out of place.

Finally, I spot him in the back of the club: a handsome, clean-cut man delighted to see me. After our warm hug, he held up two glasses of champagne. He was my hero. This was first-date magic.

Best way to describe him: a total cutie pie. Attentive, sweet, affectionate, and confident. We spent the evening tucked away in a back booth inventing all kinds of futures for the two of us to have together. I'm grateful for this man.

So what happened?

We dated a handful of times but found that we wanted different things in a relationship.

~~~~ ~~~~ ~~~~

So, friends, what have we learned thus far?

Photos are (initially) the most important piece of your profile. (Did you notice I didn't start with your profile summary or tell you whether or not you should show your income in the pull-down option?) Photos sort you out or sort you into the "Huh . . . maybe . . ." pile, and the importance of that can't be overstated or overlooked.

Next let's see what will move you from a "maybe" to a "hell yes, I gotta get me some time with her!"

10

How to Write a
Winning Online Profile

Your profile homepage is valuable real estate. It highlights your personality, sets you apart from other women, and catches his attention with your originality and points of common interest. Daters want to know: Is she attractive? Is she my flavor of person (fun, smart, quiet, serious, decisive, etc.)? Are we compatible (at least for a first date)?

We often craft our profile into the whole wife/partner package. We advertise ourselves with the endgame in mind. Some of us state that our dating purpose is to be married with three kids and have a white picket fence. This is intense, and reading it can make a guy feel like you're trying to lock him in before "hello." Right now your future date wants to know whether or not you are cute, interesting, and possibly fun. Use your online profile headline to make your point. (Men love it when we get to the point.) Show your unique flavor in the first five words.

A common complaint I hear from women is, "Men who are online are only interested in fun. They aren't serious. I'm looking for my partner. No one is talking about that online. They're all players."

If you share this complaint, you might consider that you're looking at this from the wrong perspective. You're approaching online dating by only visualizing the end, and in doing so you're missing the start. Men understand that online dating is one vehicle to connect him with a woman he wouldn't have access to in his world. And when he connects with her, he wants to move that online meeting into a real-life date. And on that date he's going to see if he likes her and finds her attractive, charming, and fun. Because when men marry, it's to someone they find attractive, are charmed by, and consider fun to be with.

Fun comes first, actually. They are taking the dating process one step at a time. Men understand that finding out what you like to do and what you stand for is important information to gather before they whip out a diamond and kneel down on one knee.

When men are looking for fun, they aren't shallow; they're smart. They're taking this process one baby step at a time. We could take a page out of their book here.

I have interviewed more than fifty men on this subject. I asked the question, "What do you think of a woman who talks about wanting to be married in her online profile?" I followed up with, "What do you think about a woman who describes under 'requirements' what her married life will look like when she meets her husband—i.e., number of children, homeschooling, etc.?" The majority of men said it was downright scary, too much, or variations on "Geez, can I buy her a cup of coffee first?" For example, one man said, "I'd like to know her name (beyond her handle) before we talk about how many kids she wants."

When we lay it all out—the wedding dress, homeschooling, and the rest of our happily-ever-after vision—right there in the introduction we can seem like we have bad judgment. These things are important elements of a partnership to explore but they are not first-impression material. There's something to be said for letting things unfold naturally. Show him who you are as a person before you show him who you are as a wife.

Be Brief and Get to the Point

I've noticed that short, to-the-point profiles are more attractive to men than they are to women. We women tend to want to know more up front and thus find longer, more detailed profiles more intriguing, whereas men tend to view longer profiles as too wordy or distracting.

To guys, less is more.

Instinctually, women crave detail. We like a good story and want the whole history. Most men don't. My dating profile was too long. It told stories. Guess who I attracted? Writers (wordsmiths who love a story).

Most men don't like all that detail the same way women do. Even if you're extra cute, if your profile is extra long he probably won't read it all the way through. But he will ask you out based on your photos and the first few sentences you wrote. Let's say that on your date, he asks you a question you answered in your online profile—below where he stopped reading. You might feel insulted that he didn't read your profile. This might make you think he's shallow. Here's a better approach: instead of writing a long profile and then being annoyed when he doesn't read it, if you can help yourself, keep your profile free of extraneous details and lengthy descriptive paragraphs. I failed at this at first and am here to tell you: you can do better.

So where do you need to trim? Topics that don't lead to points of connection. If you're talking about your love of gardening and that's something you enjoy doing alone, don't take up precious real estate with this activity.

Create a Positive Profile

Keep it upbeat. The reason online dating is not just a bunch of pictures is that people read (some of) the content you work so hard to provide (as long as it's not novel length). They're looking for personality, one that would match what they hope to find. Some are looking for a sense of humor; others are looking for compassion or a sense of adventure or nurturing and mothering skills. All are looking for women with compatible interests and values and a woman who is comfortable in her skin and happy in her life.

Show who you are by stating what you're passionate about. Who's your underdog? Talk about the things that make you happy. What do you love about your life? And yes, if you're comfortable with it, throw in a little sexy. Nothing sells more than self-confidence.

Be Unique

"I love walks on the beach."

"I'm adventurous and love to travel."

"I love to cook, dance, hike, camp, Rollerblade, and rock climb."

"I can go from jeans and a T-shirt to formal cocktail attire in the same day."

"I'm loyal to my family and friends. Family and friends are very important to me."

If you use any of these lines, congratulations, you sound just like everyone else, and he's read your profile a hundred times before he got to you. Avoid creating that same generic profile. Put your real self into it and it will entice others to want to contact you. I've been to the beach, and I fully expected to see twenty-four million Match.com consumers walking it.

Go ahead, talk about the beach but make it unique: "It's a little-known fact that temperatures on San Francisco's Ocean Beach can be in the high sixties in January. Hardly anyone thinks of going to the beach in winter, and when I visit, it's fantastic! Mild sunshine and enormous waves. It's me and Mother Nature having a little face-to-face time . . . join me?"

Love to travel? Do you need your mate to love traveling too? Instead of saying, "I love to travel," and repeating it under "Looking for . . ." write it in the "we" section and paint him a picture where he can see himself right next to you.

"We enjoy the Galapagos Islands. Swimming with ginormous sea turtles, napping in the sunshine, and eating up summer novels." I don't know about you, but I'm in. I'm packing a bag and my passport is in my purse, so let's go. When you say, "I love to travel," without painting a picture, he thinks travel is a top priority for you. Nonstop travel. Travel a week out of very month. He might think, "Can I afford to pay for our travel every month?" A man will pass you by because he wants you to be with someone who can make you happy, and he can't afford your ideal lifestyle.

As you think of what makes you unique, consider these questions:

What's impressive or different about you or your life story?

What's influenced your life choices, goals, and direction?

What sets you apart from your single, dating sisters out there?

The "I'm Looking For . . ." Section

We use the "I'm looking for . . ." section for vetting purposes. Our instincts compel us to describe as many desirable characteristics as we can to help us weed out the ones who aren't that.

"I'm looking for a masculine, spiritual, funny, transformed man who's a good communicator. He should be attractive, fit, and financially responsible/comfortable, and must like the outdoors and dressing up to go out. He should be a calm, fun, spontaneous man of integrity. He should be honest and open, and he must love my dog."

Whoa there.

If I had my way, the only thing we'd all write in this section is, "I'm looking for the right match for me." Because you won't be able to vet for the things you really need in a mate by using the descriptors. Will he have your back? Will he understand where you're coming from? Will he be able to comfort you and make you feel safe? You can't tell any of that by slapping a string of words together in the "I'm looking for . . ." section.

While we are talking about what you're looking for, for the love of God, please avoid using the phrase "I'm looking for someone who's open and honest." Guess what: after 121 dates, I can attest that nearly every man I went out with was open and honest (okay, maybe not about his height). Asking for a man to be "honest" is a bit of a backhanded insult. You might as well say, "I'm looking for the rare honest man because the bulk of you are liars." And putting "open and honest" in there won't change who you're attracting. People aren't reading that line and thinking, "Oh, crap—can't date her. I'm a withholder and a liar." The ones who lie? Yeah, they're going to reach out and lie about not lying.

Most people are open and honest if you create a safe environment. What do I mean by "safe"? Not making someone feel wronged, judged, or shamed for speaking their truth. My partner, Dave, is an over-sharer. There's something spectacularly intimate about being with an over-sharer when you're the safe place for hearing (almost) anything.

Be True

Speaking of lying, be honest yourself. No one wants to start a worthwhile relationship with lies or half-truths. Sisters, this includes your age. I understand you may be tempted to lower your age or choose a smaller body type that doesn't belong to you so you fall in the "right" search category for men. If you say you're thirty-nine and you're really fifty-six or you state you have an "average" body and you're a BBW (big, beautiful woman), guess what: He's gonna find out on your first date and his reaction, justifiably, may not be pretty.

When men lie, they usually lie about their height and age. When women lie, we often lie about our age and size. In all cases, this isn't pleasant for the one deceived, and it certainly isn't pleasant for the one who stretched the truth, when that disappointed look registers on their date's face.

Some of you don't answer truthfully in the online questionnaire to optimize placement in other people's searching preference (so you'll show up in their 25–39 range), but right there in the first line of the essay portion of your home page, you'll tell the truth. You say, "I'm the youngest fifty-six-year-old you will ever meet. I have the body of a thirty-nine-year-old. I didn't want to be ruled out of your search preferences." This is a no-pass for most people. When I asked Dave about this he said, "Let me get this straight. A woman says she's looking for an honest and open relationship and she's going to start it by lying to me? That would be a deal-breaker for me. It's not the age; it's the lie. I haven't met her yet and she's already trying to trick me or lie to me? No, thank you."

Many women believe that less attention is paid to them online when they are older, and that might be true. But that doesn't mean there's less *quality* attention. All attention isn't amazing, you know. And for the record, I know tons—and I mean dozens upon dozens— of women in their fifties and sixties who receive plenty of attention (more than they can handle) from their factual online profiles. Authenticity is irresistible.

After that lengthy moral lecture on honesty, I'm not quite sure how to break this to you, but . . . I lied. Yep, through my entire online dating experience, my "relationship status" stated "divorced" when I wasn't yet legally divorced. Because of a serious illness in my twenties, I was uninsurable for years. Once I could obtain insurance, we filed the paperwork.

When I was dating, I had a third-date rule: that's when I confessed to my date the details of the situation. I found it helpful to lead with, "The romantic part of our relationship ended in the summer of 2002." Fortunately, the men were always understanding about it.

Deal-Breakers and Timelines

The online sites help you filter deal-breakers by giving you options about things like smoking or the consumption or tolerance of alcohol or drugs. You can filter by whether or not you both want to have children and how many. Oftentimes we lead with the whole "I'm a great partner" package because that's what we want to attract, but it's a mistake to only date those who want a relationship right now. I caution you against using timing as a deal-breaker.

When I was dating, I was looking for my partner. My husband or partner or whatever he was going to be was someone I was looking for now, and I wanted him to be ready to commit to me fairly soon. I had no baggage from past relationships; I knew who I was, what I wanted to provide, and who I was looking for (for the most part).

Now, what set me apart from other women in their thirties and forties is that I didn't want children. And I'd been married before, so I didn't think of marriage as a requirement; a committed partnership would do just fine. This made me ever so slightly more chill than many of my single sisters. I wanted to reflect this in my profile. So I wrote this statement on my profile page:

"I'm looking for my partner, but I'm willing to date casually until he shows up."

That's what I said.

What I meant was, "I'm looking for my partner, but I'm willing to hang around and date you casually until you realize that you want to be my partner."

Yeah, I didn't say what I meant, and thank God! Dave (Date #121) read my profile as, "I'm looking for my partner but I'm willing to date casually until he shows up," and said to himself, "Cool. I can date her casually until her partner shows up."

Dave was fresh out of a twenty-four-year marriage and was not looking for partnership. Committing to a woman was the last thing on his mind. Yet by our second date we were falling in love, and there was nothing casual about us. Within ten months we had a commitment ceremony and the following week we moved in together.

Wait . . . the expert dater dated the newly divorced guy? What? All I can say is keep reading. I have a lot to say about the newly divorced guy.

Back to the timing thing: When we limit who we date based on them being "ready," we're not allowing for miracles to happen. We're not allowing for serendipity and for the magic of what can be an amazing match when the right two people meet. It took me 121 first dates to find Dave, so I easily could have missed my partner because he was in a different place than I was when we met.

You get to have your very own preferences and deal-breakers. Don't let anyone tell you otherwise. Men may try to convince you you're being unreasonable because you're refusing a date with him when he falls outside your parameters. Take age, for example: You are not ageist if you have a personal preference for an age bracket you'd like to date within, older or younger—it's your preference. Now, if you were an employer and you were discriminating against hiring someone based on their age, that's a different story. But we're talking about dating here. If you prefer to date older or younger, that's for you to decide, and let no one shame you. I see it often, this anger over age ranges—more from women than from men—but we all are free to choose who we're attracted to and who we feel comfortable with, so let's grant each other that, shall we?

My personal preference is older men. Although I'm awed by the ladies who can date with cougar pride, I'm not suited for the role of cougar. It just makes me uncomfortable. I need to feel like I'm the prize, not like I'm winning a prize, and a young man only makes me feel really old. But because I'm an adventurer, I tried.

Here's a fun date where I bent the rules a little.

Date #45
Super-Cougarific Me

Setting: On a docked boat, San Rafael, CA

Laptop in hand, I slumped into the oversized chair next to my bed. I curled up in just the right way where my laptop fit snugly in between my crossed legs. Did I really need to power it on to Match.com? After tonight's failed date, it might be a better idea to flatten myself out on the bed and submit to crap-reality TV. But it was only 10:03 PM; I had a pinky-nail's worth of life still left in me.

"You have mail." Thank you, Match.com. A tall, cute young man, allegedly ten years my junior, appeared to the left of a message he'd sent. "Why not?" I responded and spurred a real-time chat. By 10:30, he made a bold move and said, "I'll come to your town. Meet me now."

"Fine." I was already date-ready and could leave my house with very little effort. At 10:50, we met in the center of town, and every place around us had already closed except for one divey bar he wanted to avoid, and that was probably the right thing, because this six-foot-four child was nowhere near his thirties. I'm not certain his ID would have gotten him through the door. I am super-cougarific.

After visiting several closed locations, he said, "I know a place. Trust me?"

"Sure. Why not?" I mean, we were already out and I was already committed. I followed his car with mine to a darkened marina the next town over. He signaled me to park in the visitor parking for the nearby residents, and I did as he said.

We met between our parked cars, and he hugged me hard and said, "Okay, here's the plan. See those homes over there?"

I looked over at the multimillion-dollar homes, each with their own private boat slip and San Francisco city view. I nodded.

"My dad lives in that third house there. He's out of town. We're going to use his boat to hang out and have a drink."

Stunned, I had a rush of excitement and fear distinctly familiar. When I was fourteen, I would sneak out of the basement of my parents' home so I could hang out with friends. We'd run around and do things we probably shouldn't have been doing, in places we probably shouldn't have been.

I heard my grandmother's voice in my head: "You have no business being out after midnight. Nothing good happens after midnight." And there I was, just minutes before that "nothing good" hour, holding the hand of a boy, tiptoeing across his father's lawn, and trying not to sink into the grass with my stiletto heels as we headed for the side gate.

My date fumbled with the latch as quietly as possible, struggling to open it. All at once the oversized gate flung forward, with my date running to catch it before it made a loud crashing sound. I could see by his need for silence that we were not welcome visitors. We were, in fact, two kids (well, sort of) out after dark, somewhere where we

didn't belong, and strangely I admired him for it (while simultane-
ously doubting my own good judgment).

He steadied me in my six-inch heels along an uneven rock path
leading to the vessel. He hopped onto the massive white boat and
then helped me in. This stunning floating meeting-and-office space
made me question what the difference is between a boat and a yacht.
I couldn't tell what I was on, but it was lovely. And cold.

Date #45 rummaged through his father's liquor selection and
settled on a nearly full bottle of scotch. Without saying a word he
poured us each a glass, and as he handed me mine, I knew it was
no use telling him I wasn't a scotch drinker. I made an exception
this one time. We sat, whispering, laughing, and sipping our scotch.
He put his arm around me and kissed me lightly—until we heard a
noise.

Our focus shifted, and the remaining time on this fancy boat
was squandered by trying to determine where the noises were coming from and if, in fact, we were going to get caught. Let's face it: part
of me wanted to be caught. If his dad was not out of town and if he
were single, he certainly would have been more age-appropriate.

So what happened?

He asked me out over and over again. He was persistent. I always
said no. I don't have many rules, but I do have one called the "uterus
rule." And it goes like this: If you're young enough that you could have
come out of my uterus, you don't get to put anything of yours near it.

11

How to Find Your Mate Online

Nothing would bring me more pleasure than to tell you that all you have to do is take a cute photo, slap some words together by following my guide, sit back, and watch those compatible matches roll on in, and in twenty-four hours your inbox will be stuffed with men clamoring to meet you. Alas, my loves, it doesn't work that way.

I would also like to tell you that all the highest quality and most qualified people you date (and that I have dated) are the ones who do the contacting. Nuh-uh.

When I first put up my profile, I crossed my fingers and prayed he'd find me. And if he made the first move, that would make things so much easier because I would truly know that he was seeking me out and that I was his type—that I was what he was looking for (at least on paper).

That sounds good and all, but when it comes to online dating, it doesn't work that way for the majority of us. We have to do the searching, and we have to reach out. Of the great guys I met online, I'd say I reached out to 80 percent of them and only 20 percent reached out to me. (I reached out to Dave.)

To get the most out of the experience and find the kind of partner you're looking for, you're going to have to put in some work. Use your own search criteria via the categories your online dating company provides to filter and narrow down the pool. Consider looking for men who are like you or who at least share your point of view about life.

Your best friend has morals, ideals, standards, goals, dreams, plans, and a way of seeing the world similar to yours, right? Wouldn't you want your mate to be your best friend or at least something close to that? As you read profiles, look for qualities, goals, and attitudes that are aligned with who you are and where you are in life. Find someone you can talk to day to day versus the guy who's good-looking, tall, and has nothing in common with you.

I found I could date outside my "type," but I couldn't date outside my "tribe." Shared or complementary ways of seeing the world will foster respect in a relationship. The phrase "Oh, me too!" coming from your date makes him a little bit hotter and makes the connection between the two of you solidify faster and stronger. Consider it sexy when your date agrees with you, compared to the one who looks like your type but has a perpetual perplexed look on his face throughout dinner or drinks. You're not doing anything wrong, nor is he—he's just not your mate. If you can't make it through a conversation without feeling tense, disconnected, or like you're working too damned hard, maybe he's just not in your tribe.

You've heard the phrase "opposites attract," right? It's true! They do attract. Would you like to know why your body will flood itself with dopamine and testosterone (two hormones found in a surge of sexual chemistry)? To make a baby. That is it. That is all. That is the biological imperative. And guess when it's the most intense. When you're ovulating. Yep, when you're most likely to conceive a child, your drive will attempt to thrust you in front of the most masculine man you can find (and bed). It's a good thing we have free will, huh? (Mostly).[8]

The same thing will happen when you kiss. Your DNA and his DNA are jumping up and down and around in each other's mouths, doing a happy dance when your DNA has different components from the other. This is also the work of instinct—the design of human beings trying to make the biggest, strongest, healthiest baby ever. One with genes so different that the baby's immune system has a better shot at fighting off anything and everything bad.[9]

Your instinct to procreate is hardwired and doesn't care about who's actually the best long-term mate for you. It picks for you based on chemistry, not compatibility. It sometimes has nothing to do with the quality of your life, your resonance with this person, or your aligned life plans, hopes, and dreams. Now, does this mean you won't have good chemistry with a person you have a lot in common with? Nope; I have hot chemistry for Dave and we are a lot alike. And I'm sure those babies we're not making would be beautiful and strong. The point of all this is to beware of "opposites attract," as this is not always a good measure for a happy life.

How to Drop the Handkerchief Online

Okay, you've found a few. They're cute, they can spell, and from what you read you feel some resonance. It's time to reach out. So drop the handkerchief—online.

Keep it simple—just a line or three based on something you found in his profile. You could give him an, "Oh, me too!" for ways you're similar. Example: "You love horses? Me too! I ride in the stables on the east side. Where do you ride?"

You can give him a compliment for something you admire. Example: "You're the executive director for an animal welfare organization? Wow! That's near and dear to my heart, a cause I support both with my checkbook and through adoption. How did you decide on that line of work?"

You could ask a question about something he said in his profile. Be sure to come from a place of curiosity instead of interrogation. Example: "You spent ten months in Argentina? Wow! I'd love to know about your experiences there. Would you ever go back?"

Did you notice I asked a question in every example?

Did you also notice that none of these examples were earth-shattering or filled with illumination, intrigue, or excitement?

The purpose of dropping the handkerchief is simply to prompt him. To nudge him a little. To let him know that in the sea of twenty-five million people online, you exist and you're interested in him. This is his cue to step in and run with what you've delivered. It's fine to say more, but don't put too much energy into it. Guard your time; this is a stranger, and his interest level in you is unknown.

Now comes the hard part. Once you've found this sensational profile, crafted the simple email, and lobbed it over the fence to him, your next step is to hide his profile. Wait . . . what? Why? Trust me. Hide it. Don't block it. Blocking it won't allow him to contact you back and defeats your attempts. But most online sites give you the ability to hide a profile of a user. Don't worry, if he writes you back, you can undo the "hide" and make him visible again.

I challenge you to get into the practice of hiding the profile after you drop the handkerchief and forget you ever wrote in the first place. Just forget he even exists. When it comes to dropping the hand-kerchief, I want you to have a memory like a dog: here one moment, gone the next. If you keep moving forward and forget about your efforts, you won't be pining away if he doesn't write you back. You won't be wondering how you could have done it better; you couldn't have because your best is your best. He's not your match. You don't need to be reminded of "not your match" every time you log on and that mean online server shows you his picture in the search results. You only care about the ones who do write back.

Let's talk about the ones who are reaching out to you.

How to Be a Considerate Online Citizen

You will receive responses from good men and you will receive responses from men acting poorly. Online interaction makes it hard to find and draw the line on what to respond to, what to ignore, and frankly, how to deal with some of the crap that comes your way.

Let's say you're in Manhattan at a newsstand. You've got your cold Perrier and your *New Yorker* magazine in hand and you're waiting to pay. A man around your age comes up behind you to wait in the queue. He says, "Hi there!" You give him a friendly smile and say, "Hello." "Lovely bracelet; it looks really interesting," he comments. "Thank you," you reply. You pay, you leave, it was a pleasant exchange.

If your friendly, near-you-for-a-good-reason guy extends himself, it's polite to reply, yes? It would have been strange if he said, "Hi there! What a lovely bracelet. It looks really interesting," and you ignored him. You can be courteous online and drop him a line back, even if you're not interested.

Next example: You're standing in line with a cold Perrier and your *New Yorker* magazine in hand, waiting to pay when the fellas from the construction site to your left start whistling and cat-calling to you. Do you give those guys that same polite courtesy? Nope. You ignore them. And the way you ignore a man like that online is by hitting that little button on the top right of your keyboard: Delete.

Ignore Cruisers

You've heard me refer to "quality" and "qualified" people, so you might be wondering what's the makeup of a nonqualified person? Ultimately, that's for you to say based on who you're searching for. But here's one that's universal: the cruiser.

The cruiser is the guy who will write you an email containing two to six words. Emails like:

"Hey, Sexy."

"You're beautiful. What r u doing?"

"Nice tits."

You know this technique (if you can call it that), whether through dating online or elsewhere. It's annoying. It is one of the many things that will make you want to stop online dating. You owe the cruiser nothing, not even a "thank you" in return. Don't let him steal any of your energy or time. Hit the Delete key and pretend he never wrote. If he writes again, block him.

Some sites let people wink. This is kind of a bullshit move, and most of the time it's used by the cruiser. But some of the time it's used by a new-to-online-dating dater or the nice guy who's shy but wants to check your level of interest. So if you're using a site that lets users wink or rank highly or show interest without saying anything, it might be worth your time to investigate. If he's a cruiser, you'll be able to tell quickly by how he's written his profile or whether or not he's wearing a shirt. In which case, you can respond (or not).

Hot Tip There's usually a box to fill out in your profile that says, "Write me if . . ." You could say, "Winks are nice, but I only respond to emails that contain more than six words." The cruiser doesn't read your profile; he'll never see this phrase. Do this for you, not for him.

Avoid Long Distance

You and I have covered this earlier. You want to give the qualified people you meet online a chance, but being too far from you by definition is not a qualified match. "Too far" is any distance I'm not willing to travel three times a week. That's my rule. What's yours? When you are serious and you're spending all your time together, you'll be commuting too. Even if he does most of the commuting, if he contracts the flu and you want to go over and help take care of him, you'll be doing all the commuting. Be realistic of your tolerance level for commuting.

One of the things that we hate about online dating is that it's frequently exhausting and we spend substantial effort on people who aren't qualified—like someone who writes you from Florida when you live in California.

Here's my long-distance response policy: You owe him nothing.

If Mr. Florida writes, "Hi. You're cute," use the Delete key. It was invented for this very purpose.

If Mr. Florida writes you a long love letter telling you that you're the one for him—and you know he's not—simply write, "Thank you for emailing me. I don't date anyone more than [insert your max mileage here] miles from my house."

If he writes you back, short or long, use the Delete key and, if needed, the Block button. You've set a boundary, and what he's just shown you in his persistence is that he's a person who doesn't respect your boundaries. Good-bye.

I'd say that the exception to this rule is if he's moving to your town. In this case, engage in conversation only when he's less than sixty days away from the move. That's my "keeping it real" rule. And even then, don't over-invest.

Mr. Florida might tell you he's rich and would like to fly you over for the weekend. Hey, if you want a wild adventure and a hookup where you have no control of your circumstances, who am I to stop you? But if you're looking for something that has a shelf life longer than three days, while the whirlwind weekend may sound tempting, consider that if he really is handsome and rich, why would he need to import a woman? You know as well as I do that every single woman in a forty-five mile radius would already be working that angle. Importing you is a flaming-hot red flag.

Dating Sites Are for Single and Married People

If you're looking for a long-term partner, avoid those who are already married. The good news is that, for the most part, married people tell the truth.

Match.com seems to be more narrowly focused on single people looking for single people. Other websites such as OkCupid have categories beyond single; however, they provide you these options to choose from so you can narrow your own search despite a myriad of different relationship-style categories. There are all kinds of people looking for all kinds of relationships, and the cool thing is that most of them will tell you right up front: "I'm in an open marriage, looking for play partners," or "I'm polyamorous looking to add another partner to my life." These folks know what they're looking for and have structures around how relationships will work. (More on this subject under "Friends with Benefits and Nontraditional Arrangements.")

If you're looking for a monogamous relationship, you can take a side trip into open-marriage- and poly-land, but keep in mind that side trips and diversions may take you out of the pool for your monogamous long-term partner, if that's who you're really after.

꠵꠵꠵

If you're not convinced that online dating is the way to go, here are my statistics. I met my 121 first dates the following ways:

- 💋 Online dating sites: 102
- 💋 In person: 5
- 💋 Through friends: 9
- 💋 Matchmaking companies: 5

Of the 121, here are my numbers on how many dates the initial ones led to:

- Just one date: 84
- Two dates: 16
- Something more: 21

My dating stats on their own show that I would have gotten nowhere without online dating. Okay, let's face it: I'd be somewhere, but it wouldn't be with my partner. Meeting men through friends and random in-person encounters gave me a grand total of fourteen men, which is just a little less than one and a half men a year for every year I was single. These are not good odds, people. Random in-person meetings work for some people, but statistically my experiences fell heavily in favor of online dating.

Now, do I want your numbers to be as high as mine? Hell no! Next we'll talk about savvy ways you can work the system to your advantage and glide through this dating process with a lot more grace than I ever had.

12

Online Dating Best Practices

When you're a brand-new online dating customer, you create a profile. Once submitted, it's on the top of the stack, and the site advertises you like you're the hottest thing to hit the dating market. Every time a new woman joins, your profile becomes slightly less popular as it's slightly less "now."

When you're logged in, you show up in front of others also logged in. When you change or update your profile content, it resubmits your profile as "new," puts it out in front of the world again, and thrusts it to the top of the profile heap.

Update often, sisters. You can make minor changes—even one word does the trick. I used to change my eyes from "blue" to "light blue" then back to "blue" again nearly every time I went online.

Use the "Hide from Search" Feature

You can avoid seeing certain profiles again by "hiding" them. If you went on a date and you weren't a good match or if you ruled him out on sight, simply hide him from showing up in your search. That way you don't have to keep seeing Mr. Complicated Facial Hair Guy or

Mr. No Shirt Guy as your future opportunities. It keeps your searches fresh and helps keep you in a positive frame of mind.

Breaking It Off Before "Hello"

How to say "no, thank you" online is a skill like anything else. Dealing with unwanted attention is a major problem, and many of us girls are programmed from childhood to be nice—often too nice for our own good. In order to avoid being rude or displeasing, you might write back, at length, when really all you need to say is a polite version of, "No. Next."

Some women don't write back. You can choose that path, but I think it's rude to say nothing in return if someone has taken the time to read your profile, compose a nice email, and pin a little hope on you (think the newspaper kiosk). I try to be a courteous dater, just like I try to be a courteous human out in the world.

More often than not, after sending my simple decline email to a man, I'd receive a short email of thanks. Most men appreciate any response at all, since most women delete after scanning his profile. (Ouch.)

My sweet friend—a totally first-rate man (now married)—told me he once wrote to forty women and not one of them even responded with a "no, thank you." It took him out of online dating for good. He closed his account and never looked back. I assumed most men wanted to hear such an acknowledgment, but on a date with #120 (age thirty-seven), we talked about this subject and his reply was, "No. Rejection is bad enough. I don't want a response at all." I was stunned. So I did what I do: I researched.

In December 2012 I asked fifty men between the ages of thirty and fifty-seven whether they preferred hearing back from a woman who was not interested in dating them or whether they preferred no response. Of the men surveyed, 85 percent wanted to hear a polite "no, thanks" so they could move on and not think about her anymore, and 15 percent thought the woman didn't owe him anything and didn't care if she ever responded. (Disclaimer: I realized [much too late] that in this particular study group, most of the men were writers and musicians. The high percentage may be skewed, as they're all committed to communication and expression.)

When I say write him back, I'm referring to the men who actually write you, not the super-dudes who think volume is an acceptable dating strategy. You know who he is: You (and every other hot-blooded female breathing oxygen out there) get his email that reads, "Hey sexxy! Wut up?" With these guys in mind, God made the Delete key.

When I was dating, I kept prewritten responses saved in a conveniently placed Word document on my computer. I'd open, cut, paste, and send. I didn't put any real thought or, more important, time into it. Don't feel guilty about employing a technique like this; your time is valuable. This is considerate to them too. I recommend writing one for as many situations you think you might encounter. Here are the ones I used on a regular basis. Ready?

He writes. He lives outside your driving-to-see-my-boyfriend range.

Dear Joe,
Thank you so much for writing to me. I don't think we're quite a match, as I'm looking for someone close—no more than thirty minutes from my city. Good luck out there!

He writes. You're not interested.

Dear Joe,
Thank you so much for writing to me. I have read through your profile and have determined we're not a match. Good luck out there!

He writes a long email. You're not interested.

Dear Joe,
Thank you for taking the time to write such a nice email.
I have read through your profile and have determined we're
not a match. Good luck out there!

You could exchange the word "match" for "fit" but that's it. That's all you need. If someone sends you a long email, you may feel compelled to write more because you think you owe him. You don't. Also, know that if you go on to comment about something he said—for instance, something you have in common—you will only end up encouraging him and you may get another email, trying harder. Keep it sweet, simple, and short.

The majority of daters appreciate a reply; some don't care. And then there are the exceptions, the few special ones who don't take it well when you say, "no, thank you." Brace yourself for the rare, biting lash out. These are the same guys you hear online-dating horror stories about. He'll write something snarky like, "You must have your blinders on. I hope you have serious regrets and think back to me when you don't find what you're looking for—over and over again. You've passed up your chance at love." Yes, this is verbatim from an email I received. Delightful, isn't he?

If you receive this guy's email, shake it off. Don't let this guy's assholic behavior stop you from being courteous to the majority of men who appreciate the contact. Delete his bullshit message, take a deep breath, and let it go. Next!

Who's Favorited Me?

I'm not a fan of favoriting. I don't advocate using it to reach out to men. However, you might want to see who's favorited you.

If a man has favorited you and you like him, drop the handkerchief and say hi, just like I did in Date #51. This date favorited me, and when I read his profile, I liked him. When I knew him better, I asked why he favorited me instead of writing me an email. His reply was, "I'm new at this, and I'm shy. I was hoping you'd write me." He got his wish. He's the inspiration for this book.

Date #51
Punk-Rock Dad

Setting: Lunch at a Thai restaurant, San Francisco, CA

Date #51 was a punk-rock dad of a tween boy. He was perfect—as in we were perfect for each other—from the first line of his Match.com profile. I found him; it was really him. I knew it. The long search was over. It was MTB.

Our lengthy emails and calls before our face-to-face were beyond promising. We'd grown up in the same cultural neighborhood, ran in the same circle of friends, and had gone to the same shows from the time I hit the Bay Area in the mid 1980s. We knew each other.

"He's cute," I whispered under my breath as I walked toward him. My future mate approached me at the same pace with a broad smile that seemed to be expanding with every step. When we met, five-foot-seven to six-foot-three, he leaned down and gave me an enormous hug. *Ahh, he likes me.*

We walked to a little Thai restaurant around the corner from his work. Lunch topics included shared pasts, teenage years, points of view, likes and dislikes. We skipped the topic of relationships, and that was brilliant. We skipped those details knowing there would be plenty of time for that later.

"May I see you again?" he asked. I looked into his eyes and saw trouble—the best kind.

卌   卌   卌

What we did right: We took the approach that we were both here and single for valid reasons, while completely omitting details of past relationships.

So what happened?

It was nonstop texting through the week leading up to date #2. We were so giddy to spend time together that we blew it with a twenty-four-hour date that included meeting five of my closest family-style friends.

Alas, there is such a thing as "too much too soon." We stopped dating after that second date. He came back around a couple of times within two years for mostly friendship reasons, but he didn't find enough of a connection with me to stick around. While we liked each other, he wound up going back to a long-term girlfriend. I can't help but still adore him, despite myself.

Part II

The First Date

You've prepped. You've primped. Your profile looks like a dream.

What's next?

That's right—the actual dates. Now that you've set yourself up for success as much as it's in your power to do so, it's time to dig in and start meeting some of those potential matches. There are a host of elements to consider here: who to pick and how, where to go, what to talk about, how to present yourself, and (most important) how to determine if your date has the kind of potential that's worth pursuing into dates two, three, and beyond.

We're going to explore all this and more, including everything from first-date etiquette to bonding hormones to what to do if you need to back out of a date faster than a Formula One racer. Start your engines, girls. It's first-date time.

13

Converting Online to the Real World

What we call "chemistry" is a combination of biological chemicals (dopamine and testosterone, to name a few) along with audio and visual cues, reactions, and responses to the way a person looks, smells, moves, and sounds, and how they remind you of subconscious things.[1] Chemistry only kicks in when you're face-to-face. It doesn't work online, through text messaging, or over the telephone—no matter how deep his voice sounds.[2]

Chemistry is not a metaphysical thing. It's more primal than that, and while it shouldn't be the focal point of your potential match, its importance shouldn't be underestimated. You won't know if the two of you have potential until you meet in person.

Where am I going with this? The point of online dating isn't to get to know someone online. The point is to make choices for coffee, lunch, dinner, tennis, or movie dates to learn if there could be more. In person. Online dating is simply a tool to help you find singles you don't have access to in your daily life.

I've said it once and I'll probably say it a hundred times more: Meet right away—I mean, as soon as possible. In three days, by the weekend, or if you're traveling, right when you come back. In my experience and from what I've seen in my coaching practice, it seems that almost every relationship formed over the telephone is over in less than one minute once face-to-face.

We try to get to know him to vet him, to see if he's our man. We want to write, text, and talk on the phone first because we want to be efficient. We think going out to meet someone is not an efficient use of our time.

So we write. And write. And write. The first email is quick—the dropping of the handkerchief only takes five minutes. But then he writes back, and we like him. Oh, do we like him. He said so many amazing things, and now we have more to lose with him, so we handcraft a perfect response. This takes forty minutes.

He writes back! Your next response takes an hour to perfect. This goes on for days. When you're not writing, you're thinking about him, and you're fantasizing about how great your life will be together. Maybe you begin to share intimate things with him, things you wouldn't share with a perfect stranger.

Then you move your "online relationship" to the phone. This usually goes one of two ways:

1. You hear his voice, you don't like it, and you rule him out. It's over. This is almost always a mistake. I nearly made this mistake with one of my dates. I heard his voice on the phone, and he sounded too effeminate for me. I almost didn't meet him. But I thought, "What the hell?" When I met him face-to-face, while he had the same voice in person, with his spirit, his essence, his whole package, he was sexy and amazing. We dated for two months until he broke my heart (but I digress).

2. You like his voice so you get to know each other even more (without meeting up in person yet). Unfortunately, since you're not face-to-face, it's not an organic conversation. And he's going to be trying to impress you (because that's

what men do), so all he'll have to draw from is his history. He'll start sharing his past, his accomplishments, tell you he's a middle child. Even if this stuff is the most interesting information in the world to you, it still doesn't boil down to real-world compatibility.

Let's say it continues to go well, at which point your fantasies about him take over and you share more personal information you would never share with a complete stranger.

Then you meet. In two seconds you see you're not attracted, he's not attracted, or both of you aren't attracted. It's over. You could have spent weeks, months (I know women who have done this), and it was all for nothing. It's enough to make a good woman want to give up on dating altogether.

So why do we do it?

Safety. You think if you get to know him on the phone and by email you can trust him. This is a false indicator of knowing someone.

You think you can prequalify him (like a bank loan) if you ask enough questions before you meet. Girlfriend, you're not going to find out the things you need to know over the phone. You'll only learn those answers over time, spending date after date with him, watching his actions match his words.

What you end up with is built-up expectations, a hope of a relationship that's not real, and a lot of time you will never get back. This is not an efficient way to date.

Do you know what *is* efficient? You guessed it: meeting face-to-face. You could go from hair and makeup to the café or wine bar four doors down from your house and be back home again in under fifty minutes. Now, that's efficient.

Toward the end of my dating experience there were many times I didn't talk to a man on the phone before meeting him, and in my experience it worked better.

I wrote to Dave. I dropped the handkerchief. He picked that sucker up and wrote me right back. I replied to his email, and in his next reply he said, "Hey, I'm new at this online thing and I don't really know how it works. Can we just meet in person on Friday?" The answer to that was yes, and so it was.

This waiting business is a trap some women fall into, and if you do it, it will make you want to give up. Don't do it. Don't build him up to be way more amazing than he really is. Don't fool yourself that you have this "solid foundation" of knowing each other before you meet. You don't.

This is my biggest complaint about eHarmony: you seemingly waste too much time answering irrelevant get-to-know-you questions before you can start to talk to your match.

I know of a well-respected dating coach who's teaching his clients the two-two-two method. He says if you want quality dates, first you have to email them two times and receive emails from them two times on the dating site. After that, move off the site email to your real email and exchange two more emails each. Next step, get on the phone and have two conversations before you set a date. He offers this as he wants to save women from a string of bad coffee or dinner dates. I understand and appreciate where he's coming from, but my real-world experience (and the experiences of many women I know) shows that this is not an efficient method, nor does it provide quality matches or a guarantee of a connection when you and your date are finally face-to-face.

Cancellations

Cancellations before a first date can happen. Your job is to not take it personally. This is another reason not to invest all that initial time before you meet. Repeat after me: "His cancelling had nothing to do with me and everything to do with him."

Why he's cancelling is not your puzzle to solve. Better now than six months into your relationship together. I know it's easier said than done, but keep moving and turn your focus to who's next.

Nothing is real until you're face-to-face at the local coffee shop.

Online Dating Can Move Fast

You have a lot of information about him and he has a lot about you from your profile. It's easy and tempting to move fast—to fall into "relationship" after the first meeting or so.

It *feels* real. It feels like the right match. Slow down, cowgirl. Make sure you've spent enough time with each other that you see you're both invested in the relationship (if that's what you two are after). Phrases of how wonderful you are or what a miracle it is to finally meet someone like you are great and all, but what you need to watch for is actual time invested. Are dates being planned? Are you being wooed? Real actions—and time—are your best predictors on how it's going to go, not words.

Hot Tip In the event that you're not able to follow my "go slow" advice, tell him what you need up front before you ever have sex with him. Tell him what you need before, during, and after (including the days that follow) for you to be in suitable shape.

We all know a woman—hell, you probably *are* that woman (I am)—who does what she wants to in the moment and finds herself sitting by the telephone the next day (or days), suffering with the voice in her head telling her she blew it.

One thing we need is a telephone call the following day. You need to feel connected, cared for, and appreciated and feel like you're still the one he wants—at the level he was pursuing you before you had sex.

Facebook and Other Social Media Outfits

Would you like to know when to friend your date? When you're really, truly, honest-to-God friends and not a second sooner. Ask yourself, "If I weren't in this romantic entanglement, would I be friends with this person?"

No friending the first week. Not the first month. Hit the Friend button either when you're in a relationship or you've moved the dating thing into a friendship. Do not friend someone you've recently met—especially if you're crazy about him. Facebook is not your friend.

It's tempting, I know, to think that after an exceptional date or two or three, friending could be the natural progression of what's next. But come on, you know who's on your Facebook feed. You've got your wacky relatives who post comments to your friends (some of whom they've never even met). You've got all those strangers you knew in high school, and a variety of miscellaneous people you don't really know who constantly post religious and political rants. *That's* who Facebook is for. Oh, wait, I forgot a category: exes, or in my case the parade of exes, who enjoy saying playful, sexual things to you on Facebook. You might not want a new guy to read these.

Say you do friend him. Guess what's next: you find out things you don't want to know about him, like he's dating other women (which is an acceptable thing to do as a single person without a commitment to one person, by the way).

You start using Facebook to catch his attention.

You get mad when he clearly has enough time to write on Facebook but he's not returning a response to the email you sent him five hours ago.

You're checking his status, posts, photos, and comments like an insane stalker.

Seriously, hold off on friending. You don't need any of that insanity until there's something more, as in exclusivity or a real, live friendship without a promise of a future together.

So where are we?

- Meet right away, for the sake of efficiency and keeping it real.
- Relying on the phone can get in the way of a relationship. You need to see him in the flesh.
- We can't ever fully vet our date in advance.
- When cancellations happen, it's him, not you.
- Pay attention to the speed of the relationship; online dating can move fast.
- Facebook isn't your friend for friending; you can't un-see something you've seen (nor can he).

Now, let's get you out into the real world and on a date, shall we?

14

Dos and Don'ts for the First Date

You agree to meet him for the first time. He was, in fact, right around the corner. Yay! You've said yes to a first date; it's lunch this Saturday. He asks, "Where would you like to go?"

And you say, "Wherever you want to go is fine."

This is frustrating—both for you and for him. He might try again by asking, "What's your favorite restaurant?" and you'll once again dodge making the final decision by saying something like, "I like everything—you choose," throwing the accountability back squarely in his lap. For some couples this goes on and on and on, every time they go out, for decades. Would you like to know why?

In the mating and dating game, he is instinctually trying to impress you and you're trying to attract him. That's it. That's the mating process. He's using everything he's got (or says he's got) to impress. You're doing everything you can to attract.

A man is taking you out because he is trying to get to know you and he wants to impress you. The main thing he wants from this date is to make you happy. (The second might be getting lucky, but we're not quite there yet.) He would like to go somewhere he'll consider satisfactory, but ultimately the point is to see you have an excellent time. So when he asks you where you want to go, he would appreciate it if you'd tell him what you like. But we often don't. Why?

One way we attract a man is by trying to please him. We think, "Be low maintenance; that will attract him," or "Don't be too much trouble." This is why we say things like, "Anything is fine."

I'm guessing anything is not "fine." If he took you to Denny's I'm guessing you wouldn't be fine with that (unless you're super into pancakes or something). Some of us restaurant snobs are not going to be too thrilled with a subpar family-friendly chain restaurant, even if the blooming onion ring is delicious. But if you're sweet and you want to be considerate of his needs and his budget, it's hard to tell him exactly what you want, especially if what would make you happy is Chez Panisse or Le Bernardin. So what do you do?

Offer two suggestions of places you like in two different price categories and styles of food, and offer him the freedom to counter. You could say something like:

"I like Zuni and It's Tops. If you're interested in either of those restaurants, I'm in. I also like trying new places, so if you want to suggest something else, I'm open to that, too."

See, now you've given him something to work with: Zuni at the higher price point and It's Tops at the lower and two styles of food. Before your suggestions, he had the whole world of food options to pick from to try to make a good first impression, and he didn't even know what you like. Do you eat raw fish? Like Italian? How about Ethiopian? Hot dogs? Are you gluten-free? You have now narrowed it down for him. He can Yelp the two restaurants and see if either works for him, and if they don't, he can find a place comparable for a counteroffer.

Providing two options is kind to him. He is now set up to win with you, which gives him confidence—he appreciates that. This benefits you too. You get to go somewhere you know you're going to like and where, for sure, you'll find something on the menu you can eat. It's what they called in the 1980s a win-win.

Hot Tip Your first date doesn't need to be extravagant. In fact, one could argue that close to free might be better. Doing something casual (read: inexpensive) will take off some of the pressure, especially since you've never met, and this is just a meet-and-greet. Getting together for coffee or a quick drink after work is popular. One of my favorite first dates was walking around an urban lake. Try hiking or walking, as long as it's a busy public trail or park. Or take advantage of something fun that your town offers, like a night walking tour, a museum event, or a gallery exhibit. Let's talk about this some more in the next chapter.

Where to Go (and Not to Go) on Your First Date

I wouldn't spend too much time thinking about where to go on your first date; doing so only complicates things and adds to your to-do list. The groovy little wine bar or cozy neighborhood coffee shop within two blocks of your house could be your spot—every time. Give the staff something to talk about. They'll grow to adore you, and they'll have your back.

One woman said, "I don't want to meet my husband in a Starbucks. Our story needs to be romantic." After two years of trying to make memorable meetings with every new stranger, she's come around to my way of thinking: I'm in favor of making that fairy-tale beginning start on date #2.

One woman said, "I have a dating plan. When I meet a man online, the first date is coffee, the second date is lunch, the third date could be dinner. We don't have sex for three months, and we don't go out of town together or do overnights for three more months." This is her strategy. You are entitled to what you need, and if you need a strategy, go for it.

You know what my first question to her was, right? "So how many men have you dated for longer than three months?"

"One . . . and it was long distance."

I'm not saying her plan was a bad one. She needs what she needs, and I don't begrudge her that. But you might notice from this example that it leaves little to no room for a relationship to grow organically. It's all strategy and no flexibility.

Working from a strategic plan or an agenda can seem manipulative and inauthentic, which is the opposite of what is attractive about us—confidence and authenticity. Her plan to date "right" might have pushed good men away.

There's freedom and power in knowing there's no "right way" to date.

Lunch Date

A lunch date is a nice, safe choice. If it's a weekday, you have the advantage of having to go back to work to graciously end a date. It's an easy route. But it can be a bit of a hindrance if you two like each other and want more time together than just an hour.

Sunday Brunch

Sunday brunch can be fun, especially if you throw in a pitcher of mimosas into the mix.

Dinner Date

A dinner date is absolutely a fine idea for the ones you think you can talk to for at least an hour—even if you two are not a romantic match.

A Film or Live Entertainment

Seeing a film or checking out some form of live entertainment is not the best first date, unless there's something out that you two are both into seeing, in which case I recommend you have dinner or a drink near the theater or venue first so you can get to know each other a bit. That way, later, when a move is made to hold your hand, you have some familiarity and a sense of whether you want to reciprocate or not.

Farmers' Market

If you live in an area with a big farmers' market, this could be a fun first date. You can stroll and talk. There's no pressure, and you can easily and naturally end the date at any time or decide where you're going to go together after that.

Walk Around an Urban Park or a Lake

Strolling around a park, a lake, or even interesting city blocks will offer beauty and relative privacy. You can hang out longer or end it early. This date gives you flexibility to change the plan gracefully.

Other Ideas

Go surfing, target shooting, bowling, fencing, golfing, go-cart racing, horseback riding, roller skating, or ice skating. Join a volunteer project, picnic in a public area, play tennis, go on a scavenger hunt, take in a concert or literary event, tour an art gallery or museum, attend a lecture or discussion . . . The possibilities are, if not endless, rather extensive. Want more? Consult your old friend Google for popular picks or unique local options.

Date Disasters: Location Edition

There's been more than one romantic comedy based on the premise of finding true love at a dog park. I'm here to tell you, I road-tested this one, and a date at a dog park is disastrous. Imagine trying to talk about how many siblings you have and what you do for a living while he's chasing after his Shih Tzu who's trying to hump a Labradoodle. Mmm . . . sexy.

Also a bad idea? Going to a live event hosted by a celebrity you have a major crush on. I went to a San Francisco book reading with Jack Boulware, writer and all-around local hero, and I couldn't focus on my date at all.

But the worst first-date idea of them all can be found in the next date, for your reading pleasure.

Date #66
The Felon

Setting: Hike and dinner at Bungalow 44, Mill Valley, CA

This guy was promising. He was six-foot-two, handsome, and gainfully employed and making a comfortable living. What's not to like?

We set up a date to hike Mt. Tam. As locals know, hiking is about the only thing we do here in the North Bay, so being off the beaten path didn't seem unusual to me. However, when I met him face-to-face something in my gut told me to change the plan. (Always trust your gut.)

"Hey, I think these shoes are giving out on me. Do you mind if we do an urban hike around the hilly neighborhoods instead?" I asked.

He was amenable. As we ascended the first slope up to the more modest homes (average market value of around $1.4 million—I know, right?!) he asked, "So, do you want to be married again? I know I'd like to be married."

"Sure, probably," I said. "I'm just looking for the right partner for me. I don't care about the paper or need the title of 'wife.' Hey, how in the world did you make it to forty-four without ever being married yourself if that's what you want?"

"I've spent the greater part of my adult life in San Quentin and various facilities around the greater San Francisco Bay Area."

Yes, ladies and gentlemen, I was on a date with a career criminal.

"What's the beginning of that story?" I asked, figuring that I might as well hear the whole tale if he was willing to tell it to me.

"When I was thirteen, I fell into a pharmaceuticals-oriented crowd. We learned that stealing expensive art pieces and selling them to antiques dealers was a lucrative way of funding our habit.

"My finest accomplishment was winning over an owner of a summer home mansion. I became his 'caretaker' and cleaned him out within a month. I went to prison for that one for a long time. I learned a good lesson."

"What lesson was that?" I asked.

"I moved on to commercial buildings, removing antiques from banks, schools and the like—prison time for this type of grand larceny is not as severe."

Oh. My. God.

An hour later as we descended the hill he asked, "Want to go to dinner?"

"Absolutely!" I said. (You just can't pay for this kind of entertainment.)

Settled into a corner table at the posh Bungalow 44, Date #66 regaled me with more stories. His drug of choice was methamphetamine; he said it brought out his creative side. As an unfortunate side effect, it led him to hear voices, a few of which told him to kill his neighbors. The voices gave him specific instructions to accomplish the task: by pumping poison toxins through their vents and cutting their electrical power. After time spent in prison for that one, he stayed with a friend—that is, until she got evicted after he cut the power in her ten-unit apartment building.

"When I quit drugs, the voices eventually went away. So I'm no longer carrying a hammer in my back pocket."

Hot Tip Don't go hiking on a first meet-and-greet date. He could be a recovering drug addict and felon who carries a hammer in his back pocket.

There is something I did right here that I could have easily gotten wrong. In that moment of meeting, I trusted my gut and changed our plans. Was it uncomfortable to tell him we weren't going hiking? Yes.

Often times our gut tells us something is off and we think "I can't tell him no" or " I can't change the plan" or even "He might think I'm judging him." We don't want to be displeasing—that's our inherent female inclination. So one part of your instinct (your gut) is trying to keep you safe, while the other part is trying to be accommodating. It's maddening. But you *should* be pre-judging him! Please, for your own safety, try not to override your own instincts. They are working to keep you safe.

15

On Your First Date

Alrighty—it's date time at last.

If this is an online date or a blind fix-up, exchange cell phone numbers before you go. Most people don't look like their pictures, and sometimes it's hard to find each other the first time. You also can't count on traffic and need to be able to reach each other if you're running late.

If you're feeling uncomfortable about giving a stranger your cell phone number, you can use a Google Voice number for free (just search online for "Google Voice"). The number rings to your phone and you have the option to turn the number off as desired. Be sure and block your caller ID, because if you don't and you call him back, your actual cell number will show up on his phone.

I didn't mind giving out my telephone number. And after 121 first dates and zero incidents of abuse, I have direct evidence that I can trust a person with a phone number. One potential problem with giving out your cell phone number is they can Google it. If you're me, they'll learn that you've written a book on dating, have been on 121 first dates, and you've written details in said book. I managed to paint myself into a pretty corner. If you're known for something you don't want your future dates to know about and your phone number is tied to it through Google, you may want to use an alternate method. It's not always easy being (in)famous.

Date #56 was supposed to meet me at 10:00 PM, and by 10:15 I couldn't find him. His photos didn't give me enough information, but I knew I was looking for tall.

A handsome man walked by me, smiled in seeming recognition, and kept going without saying a word, right out the door. Really? REALLY? You're going to walk right by me and just because I'm not your type you're not going to have the common courtesy to say, "Thank you, but no thank you?" Really?

Just to be triple-sure, I texted him as I stomped off to my car, "K—where are you?" As I pulled away from my impossible-to-find coveted San Francisco parking spot, he replied, "I'm at the end of the bar waiting for you. Where are you?" Oops. "I'm parking," I text.

We had a good laugh over it, but I learned my lessons, the first of which is to ask for a better (more recognizable) photo before setting out on a date, and second, to always program his number into my cell phone, just in case.

Once you both arrive safely and you've found each other, pick up your cell phone and say, "I'm going to shut this off. I don't want it to interrupt our date." This tells him three things:

1. You're courteous.
2. You want him to be courteous too—so he should also turn off his damned phone.
3. You're not going to use the phone for a fake emergency call later. (Note: This only works when you're not going to use your phone for a fake emergency call later. You would never do this, I know.)

One of the greatest gifts you can give your dates is the gift of your authentic self. I like to wear dresses and skirts. To show up on a first date in pants would be weird for me. Also, I don't cook—at all.

Hot Tip Don't try to be someone you're not. I tried to cook a full dinner for a first date with someone I'd known a while, Date #6. It was a disaster. I slaved over it for days, obsessed and worried (it was a simple chicken dish, BTW), and he wasn't appreciative of my efforts. I learned that from then on I was going to impress men with things I was actually skilled at, not with the things I consider a struggle.

The Secret Trick to Knowing Him

What made me a welcome first date was the way I connected with a man when we first met. I "knew" him. You can do this too. When you do, it makes you approachable, comfortable, and easy to be with. It puts him at ease and gives him the feeling you two have known each other a long time. Here's how it works:

Walk into the place as if you already know him.

Greet him as if he were one of your closest friends: casual, friendly, relaxed, connected, and genuinely happy to see him.

As you sit down together, talk to him as if you were his wife or good friend. Once you both have your coffee and you're seated, you could ask, "How was your day?" or "What happened today?" It breeds familiarity and shows you're receptive; you care about him as a whole person.

Listen. It's a way to be engaged and start the ball rolling without the "interview."

After "How was your day?" the conversation is often more organic. And the big bonus is that if he starts doing all the talking, you learn things about him (as in who he is, what he cares about, and what's important to him) right from the start.

Men hate the interview. *Hate* is not too strong a word here. They hate it. It's the checklist or line of questioning we ask so we can learn if he can measure up to our stupendously high standards. He'll tell you everything you need to know if you're willing to listen and not interrupt to change the subject. And he will tell you without your having to ask. This method for listening is slightly sneaky but seriously effective.

Another considerable outcome from "knowing him" from the start is that it builds partnership from the moment you meet. This is important to a man who's interested in someone for a committed relationship.

Be Careful with the "Know Him" Tool

If you notice partway through your evening that he's wild about you and you're not wild about him, what do you do?

First, it's not surprising—that damned "know him" strategy of having him share about his day with you worked so well he opened right up to you, felt comfortable, even fell a little bit in love with you. That can happen when they feel connected, even that fast. It feels like he's known you forever. If you don't stop it early, by the end of the date, he'll be completely blindsided when you don't want to see him again. It won't make any sense to him, and frankly, it's just a mean thing to do to somebody.

Once you know he's not your guy, you need to tweak the way you're interacting with him and as early as you can, let him know the two of you are not quite a match. Save him from the rug pull.

Shift that warm, familiar, connected energy to a different kind— one that's more flat and direct, like you're just a pleasant person who's making polite chitchat with a stranger—and then begin to wrap up the date by saying something like, "Thanks for meeting up with me. I need to be heading out soon."

Date Conversation

There are many schools of thought on what and how much to say on a first date.

Relationship expert Alison Armstrong advises daters to "state your relationship purpose" right out of the gate.[3] Right there, on your first date, be yourself and tell him what your point is for dating—your endgame. For example: "I want to be a married stay-at-home mom and have lots of babies."

Or, "I'm looking for a husband. I want to be married, buy a house with a big front porch, and live in the Hudson Valley for the rest of our lives."

Noooo, Alison, no. She tells women to do this because she did this with her husband on their first date and it worked. What's different about her situation is that her first date was not a blind date or an online date. By the time they went on their first date, Greg had known who she was for a minute. He'd seen her in action, and based on their volunteer work together he assumed he knew what she was about and what mattered to her. And the most important detail? He was already in love with her. You don't have that same luxury when you're on a meet-and-greet coffee date with Mr. Match.com.

Think about it: a date is to get to know each other. You know, like a friend. You wouldn't tell a woman you met as a new friend on your first coffee date together that you were dying to be married, have tons of babies, and be a stay-at-home mom. Okay, maybe you would. And that's not bad because you're both women and many of us love to reveal and listen to these details, but to most men, it seems a bit over the top. I mean, he doesn't even know if you own a bicycle, if you like cooking, if you're willing to travel to Ohio every Christmas to be with his family—and now he has to figure out if he is suitable to be the daddy of your children? Brakes, brakes, brakes! Remember when we talked about not including all the details of your happily-ever-after in your profile, right up front? Same situation here. This is when men say things like, "She came on like a Mack truck!" and "Speaking of marriage on a first meeting is scary!"

I tried it Alison's way—with disastrous results. I am always up for a good science experiment, even if it means blowing up the lab, so I tried it over and over. After my not-so-stellar personal results with this approach, I did a ton of research with men.

In one of my interviews, I heard the story of a man in his late thirties and looking for a wife in New York City. He was elated when the woman he'd been eyeing at the gym said yes to his dinner invitation. They'd barely slid into their seats when she announced, "I'm looking for my husband. I'm thirty-four and I don't have much time left. I want babies. So if you're not interested in that, we should leave now. I want my husband, and I'm sick of wasting time." And in that moment, the date was over.

Here's the thing: as far as he could tell, she had the goods. He wanted to get to know her and potentially give her what she was asking for, just not the first week. The abrupt and direct approach did them in.

As I mentioned before, if on my first date with Dave I'd told him I was only willing to date men who were interested in a serious relationship right now, he would have said, "Check, please." And we were never—and I mean never—casual in our dating. We were locked into the love bubble somewhere between the second and third date.

Seattle Nate, forty-six, went through a long phase of hunting for a wife. On a first date he'll give you a seven-page list of deal-breakers, hopes, dreams, and desires. So he appreciates all that information right up front. Know this: he is a rare exception. We used to joke that in our friendship, he was the chick and I was the dude.

I've learned there's something to be said for letting things unfold naturally, as one would with any new friend. You have a million other interesting things to talk about, and he does too. Your date will tell you what he's looking for if you're willing to listen for it. The answer comes out within the first or second date anyway.

Telling a man on a first date that you want a wedding ring, children, and a white picket fence (or any equivalent) so you can live happily ever after is as sexy to a man as talk of a prenuptial agreement probably is to you. Don't lead with the endgame in mind.

Your Ex, Your Terrible Boss, and Other Tales of Woe

Speaking of unthinkable things to say, you know what? He doesn't need to hear about your nightmare ex from hell on your first date together. And by the way, if you call your ex an asshole, he'll just be wondering how long it will take before you're calling him an asshole (even if your ex was a total asshole). Commiserating with him about your past relationship misfortune(s) is not a sexy move.

It's tempting to talk about your ex. You may feel compelled to give him a sound bite or two to validate your single status. It's not necessary. He assumes that you're single for valid and legitimate reasons, as he is. You don't need to say why. And you don't need to justify yourself. If he asks, you can do a quick pitch—something like, "We weren't a match, and I'll tell you more when I know you better," and then move onto another topic.

Unless one of you works or does serious volunteering in local government or is an elected official or a lobbyist, or you just want to sort your mate by his political convictions, you can save politics for another time.

Religion? If you have strongly held opinions or convictions, it's good to talk about this sooner to see if you two are compatible in your faith (or lack of it). If you're not, see if you're both tolerant of each other's points of view. Conversations about religion and politics may be one way to help you sort faster, but you may sort yourself out of his life before you were ready to go.

I didn't worry too much about taboo topics. For me, it was a bit of a sorting mechanism. On my first date with Dave, I regaled him with the story of my six-month adventure of officially excommunicating myself from the Mormon Church. About a month later he told me that when he met me he knew he wanted to sleep with me, but that when I was partway through that story, he realized he wanted to get to know me.

Some of the best dates I ever had were ones where my date and I talked about sex, religion, *and* politics. If that happens for you, you may want to address it as it's happening. For example, say: "I can't believe we've gotten this far into religion. Yes, I'm from Utah and all, but isn't this a taboo date topic? I'm comfortable with talking about this, but I'm also happy to switch topics. We could talk about your new job instead. Which would you rather talk about?"

Now, if you're starting to get heated, I wouldn't even ask—I'd switch over to another topic. You could say, "Ooh, we've stumbled upon something I'm not quite comfortable talking about yet. Can I share the highlights of my recent trip to New York instead?"

Stay clear of emotional topics in email and in person with someone you have never met. Talking about your terminally ill sister is too much for a stranger to handle. And even if he can handle it, it's not the cleanest way to start a relationship. If things in your life are too painful to not talk about on a first date, consider that you're not ready to date right now.

Who Else Are You Seeing?

"So, are you dating a lot of other guys?" Your date might ask this question. It's a rude question. Please don't ask him about the other women he's dating. Would you like to know why? Being single doesn't have all that many privileges as compared to a couple's privilege. But here's one: being single means you have autonomy. You get to do what you want, with who you want, whenever you damn well feel like it. And it's nobody's business.

Whose business? Nobody's business.

Single means single and you're available. There's nothing wrong with dating more than one person; you're sorting for your partner, and you don't want to try to sort in a pond of one. You won't have the discernment you need if you do that, and neither will he. Here's what you can say to, "So are you dating a lot of other guys?"

"I'm single and dating, yes."

He might ask, "Well, how many?" and you can say, "I'm sorry, that's private, unless I'm misinterpreting what you're asking me. Are you asking me to be exclusive with you?" That should end the line of questioning. If he persists, he's telling you something about who he is. Pay attention, because you've just set a polite boundary and he might be about to trample all over it with something like, "But I need to know who else you're dating." Um, no, he doesn't. It's your private life, you're entitled to it, and you can tell him I said so.

Consider this for your next question: What about sleeping with more than one person? I leave this super-fun decision to you to decide what's right for your life. However, when it comes to sharing that information, the same rules apply: single is single, and you owe no one anything unless you have an exclusive deal with them. (Just remember to practice safe sex, friends.)

Zip It

Resist the urge to overtalk about yourself; try to listen. Everyone has a story to tell. On some of my more significant dates, my biggest regret was that I talked too much. This happens when one is excited about their date. You want him to know you so he'll pick you. You talk and talk, and sometimes you talk about ridiculous things—and when I say "you," I mean me. See, I made this mistake over and over just so you don't have to. (Yeah, yeah, you're welcome.) Allowing him to talk will give you valuable sorting information (just like I did for them when I talked their ear off).

So, why did I keep making that mistake? I think it's because when we meet someone we really like, the brain just wants to take the shortcut. You know he's it, so you switch to catching him by impressing him, and all curiosity about who he is ends . . . and that's objectifying.

Pets

I have a dog. I love my dog. Her name is Lilly. I also call her Lilly-Bee, or The B. If I could bring her every damned place I go, I would. Yep, I'm one of those goofy dog moms. She's a Catahoula Leopard dog, or at least that's what they told us when I fetched her from the pound. She has a sad story. She almost didn't make it out alive. Would you like to hear the story of how I got her?

No, of course you wouldn't. You're bored by this story already.

Don't do this to your date. Don't talk about your pet obsessively. Your date doesn't care or love her the way you do (not yet anyway), and now he is forced to listen, feign interest, and muster fake enthusiasm; otherwise, you won't like him for not loving your dog. Don't be that jerk.

Dating Sucks

Don't talk about what a drag it is to date unless you tell one hilarious, well-crafted tale you've prescreened with your best friend. Don't just go whipping one out after two glasses of wine. You don't know where or how that thing might backfire.

Self-Deprecation

Talking him out of thinking you're hot, smart, interesting, or an exceptional candidate (if you like him) is so not cool. Don't shoot yourself out of the sky, ladies. You deserve better from yourself.

Other Men Can Wait

I know I don't have to tell you this, but I may as well mention it anyway: don't check out or flirt with other men when you're on your date. Wait, girl! Whether you like him or not, you owe him the respect to keep your attention focused on him. And if your perfect partner happens to also be dining in the restaurant while you're there, karma will put you two together at a different time, in a different place.

What's Your Part and What's Not Your Part

While it's fine to be entertaining, it's not your job to be sure he's enjoying himself. One way we compensate for another's seeming lack of enjoyment or a gap in the conversation is by trying to hold up both sides of the conversation. I unconsciously did it through many of my dates. It's exhausting and not fun—not at all. When you're on a date, watch for overcompensation and make adjustments so that you're only doing your part.

Dance in the conversation and flow with your date. If you like him, your part is to be inviting, but don't be the one to lead. Let him lead. Not out of any old-fashioned cultural script, but when you let a man lead, you'll be able to see if he shows up for you willingly and eagerly. You want to see where he's leading you to. If you're the one leading, you may question if he's interested or if he's simply following.

The next date is an example of where I wasn't careful at all. Enjoy.

Date #101
Taboo Topics and Broken Rules
Can Still Lead to More

Setting: Writers with Drinks at Make-Out Room;
Doc's Clock; and Beast and the Hare,
San Francisco, CA

Anyone who wants to meet me can usually find me at Writers with Drinks. It's a literary event that happens the second Saturday of every month at Make-Out Room, a quirky little venue in the Mission District of San Francisco.

Originally, I went to listen to writers read their work. After my third time, I realized that I don't go there for the authors' readings; I'm there for the host, Charlie Jane Anders. She's one of the quickest, brightest, funniest women I know. Like most of San Francisco, I kinda have a girl crush on her. Charlie stuns us with her fine sense of fashion and newest hair color whilst she spins elaborate fake bios of writers right before introducing them to the crowd. She is a powerhouse.

Writers with Drinks is a test date. If a man can't hang here, he probably isn't going to be able to hang with me. The writers are irreverent, bold, edgy, and usually read from their books on sex, BDSM, or lesbianism, and sometimes on lesbian BDSM sex, as was the case this evening.

On Twenty-Second Street, in front of the old marquee above Make-Out Room, I stalled to read his texts to see he was already inside and had covered my admission fee and secured two seats. A moment later, a new text arrived: "You'll be able to spot me easily—I'm the one with the jitters." This new information began to calm my trembling hands and wobbly legs. How could this be? How could I be so nervous? I reminded myself, I've got this. I've done this before, a hundred times already.

I spotted him holding our two coveted barstools. He bought me a drink, and for the first few minutes he seemed unnaturally quiet—it was nerves. Sweet. As we both relaxed, we exchanged a handful of stories before the show started. I found him smart, insightful, interesting, and really funny. We both laughed at the same things when often other people didn't. Perfect.

He looked like Hugh Laurie—nearly every woman's go-to crush (in my opinion). He was so my type, I considered not even attempting a date—chemistry is like crack, after all. My saving grace was that he didn't sound or act like Hugh Laurie. Date #101 had his own personality, which gave me a shot at being myself instead of some odd, contorted version of something that might resemble me.

His formative years were spent on the East Coast, accent included. It was slight until he got a bit animated telling stories, at which point it filled out. When he talked about this mother I wondered if we were sitting in her kitchen.

As the show wrapped up, I made quick introductions to old friends of mine—the bar owner, the sound man, and others. We also got to say hi to Charlie Jane, a big highlight. As everyone poured out of the club, we realized we weren't done with each other.

Our next stop: Doc's Clock. A woman looking much like Susan Sarandon's twin sister with a little bit of Shelley Long thrown in for good measure asked what she could get us to drink to start us on what turned out to be the storytelling portion of the evening.

As we'd stumble onto taboo topics, I'd turn tentative and back off. Finally, he told me to knock it off—to trust him. Maybe, just maybe I could trust him not to judge me for what I was about to say. So I went for it. Often. We had all kinds of treacherous first-date conversations that should have killed any potential for a second date, and it all turned out fine.

It worked because I trusted him. Okay, maybe I didn't know if I could trust him, but I figured I could trust Hugh Laurie. We talked, looked into each other's eyes, and kissed, talked, looked at each other, and kissed some more. We repeated this cycle several times. I loved my life. Eventually, I looked at my phone to check the time: 1:30 AM. In horror, I realized the parking garage that I'd used closed at midnight. BART stopped running at midnight as well.

I asked, "Can you drive me to my friend Melissa's house? She has four children. I'll probably wake them all up. She won't mind, though."

"I could, but I'd rather you stay with me. Don't worry—we won't have sex. I just want more time with you," he replied.

What's a girl to do?

In the morning, he told me I looked pretty without makeup. No one had ever said that to me. In that moment, it felt like one of the greatest compliments I'd ever gotten.

He was kind enough to lend me his red Converse sneakers, because I couldn't bear putting on my knee-high six-inch-heel stripper boots for the Walk of Shame—which we renamed the "Walk of Pride"—on a Sunday morning. So in my short black dress, black tights, and borrowed red Chucks, I fit right in with all the cool kids of the Mission District on a late Sunday morning.

After a tasty breakfast of chicken and waffles, he walked me to my car, kissed me good-bye, and we parted ways—him with lipstick on his lower lip and me with borrowed red sneakers.

       |||| |||| ||||

Broken Rule #1: We discussed taboo topics I would normally save for much, much later—things like the fact that I lead workshops about relationships and sex, that I teach dating classes, that he was first date #101, and that I dance on a pole at the Power Exchange.

Broken Rule #2: I stayed the night at his house—on the first date (yes, I did). Hey, I was stuck. Don't judge, and if you do, judge how pretty I look in the morning without any makeup.

So what happened?

Several more dates and we converted to "just friends." I was nuts about him (still am). He wanted to move to China. I never want to do that (not that he was asking).

There's plenty to chew on, plenty of guidelines to follow, and many a pitfall to avoid on a first date. But ultimately the most important thing to remember is to be yourself. Authenticity is completely charming. Even if you realize twenty minutes in that you're still talking about your cat. Even if you accidentally reveal an embarrassing story. Even if you're chatting his ear off because you're overly attracted to him. Give yourself a big, fat break. It's all good, and it's just a part of the experience of dating. It will be fun fodder for you and your girlfriends over coffee next week. If you did your best (even with a blunder or ten) and showed up as your unique self, you did it right.

16

You Need to Connect, He Needs to Deliver

Now you know how to do it: Displaying confidence but also keeping it open-ended, you say, "I like Zuni and It's Tops. If you're interested in either of those restaurants, I'm in. I also like trying new places, so if you want to suggest something else, I'm open to that too."

Since your friend, Maggie set you two up, you say "sure." Then he says, "Wow, Zuni. I haven't been there since it opened. Let's go there. I'll pick you up; no need for us to both pay for parking."

He arrives outside your apartment, has double-parked, and rings your doorbell. You open the door, and there he stands in front of you—flesh and blood, the real man at last—and in one instant the most important thing you're looking for is to feel that certain non-verbal connection. It's been a weeklong text-messaging frenzy since you two were introduced via email, and you want to see if that spark's going to translate to in-person wow—that tingling something you feel when a physical connection has been made. Okay, pretty good so far.

You jump in his gray Honda that's blocking the slow lane, hazard lights flashing, and then he jumps in the driver's side and points the car toward the restaurant. You immediately start asking questions.

"This is a nice car. Is it new?"

"How did your presentation go at work?"

"What else happened this week? Tell me about. . ."

You're noticing he's not that responsive. He seems distracted. Your inner critic opens its loud mouth and starts in on you at top speed. *Is he agitated with me? Maybe he doesn't like me as much as I thought. Oh no.* So you try a few more questions. They don't go any better. You two just don't seem to be connecting.

Hmm . . . maybe he's a bad driver and needs to focus on driving. You're ever so slightly irked and fall silent until you arrive at the restaurant. Once you're inside, you try again.

"So, you came here when it opened. Did they have this fancy bar section built then?"

"Uh, yeah, I think so."

Okay, good sign. You start firing more questions at him, but he still seems distracted. In fact, he's not paying any attention to you. He seems to be more concerned with what the cute host is doing. Ugh, is he *that* guy? Or is he just trying to catch her attention to let her know you're there and you have reservations? She's cute, especially in that tiny vintage dress, lace stockings, and Mary Janes. You look at your own shoes and your inner critic decides to pick that moment to tell you that you should be more stylish.

You settle in at your table, menus in hand, and you say, "What have you had here?" He mutters something about the burger but they don't serve it until 11 PM, and now you're deflated. You have tried to connect with him and clearly this just isn't going well. This is not the same guy you've been texting with all week. He seems to be disengaged and focusing on everything around him but you.

(Sigh.)

What gives?

Your first priority is to make a connection—physical attraction and more importantly, a personal connection—while his is far from it. In most cases his priorities are focused in a different way: "Get it done, deliver, and don't screw it up." Finding where you live and dealing with the nonexistent parking in your urban neighborhood was producing a result. Putting you into the car and driving to the restaurant safely was producing a result. Getting you to your table: also delivering a result.

Most guys aren't great multitaskers. Ever notice how men tend to focus on one result at a time? So his sole focus to deliver those results leaves very little space for chitchat or eye-to-eye connection. From his perspective, that can happen once the two of you are safely at the restaurant, at your table, items chosen, and ordered. That's when he can pick his head up, meet your gaze, and say, "Hi. How've you been this week?" But by then, you've written him off. From where you're sitting, clearly he was miserable for that whole first forty-five minutes. The spark is gone. By this time, you're ready to leave but he's just getting started. It's a common mistake people make: not understanding what's happening for the opposite sex, when most women are driven by a completely different set of priorities than men and vice versa.

So how do you deal with this different communication style? How do you prevent this experience from happening to you (again and again)? Start by understanding that when a man is focused on producing a result (in this instance, getting the date up and running), he probably won't be paying much attention to you at that moment. It doesn't mean he likes you less. In fact, I'd consider it a tip-off that you and the date are important to him.

Don't pass judgment on compatibility until you've actually had solid time together, where you're talking uninterrupted over the meal. Learning to understand your instant instincts—that flesh-and-blood feeling when you first meet (more on this in the next chapter)—and then to give the personal connection time to flourish through conversation when both parties are comfortable, present, and ready is very important. And for the love of God, if you like where you are, stay put. A venue change will cause that same disconnect until you're settled at the new place. I used to think progressive dinners (moving locations for every course) sounded fun until I learned this about men through Alison Armstrong. Now progressive dinners just sound like torture.

Here's a success story where knowing about this very topic made it so.

Date #31
Staying In

Setting: My house (that's right, my house), Sonoma, CA

The plan was to have dinner at one of Sonoma's finest restaurants, but this date was a bit tricky to construct. His commute from San Francisco to Sonoma at 5:00 PM on a Friday in winter rain could take anywhere from an hour and a half (optimistically) to three hours (realistically), and I knew it.

That's a lot of effort for a first date. We had much in common, including a handful of friends. I took this as a sign. Since he was willing to put in the effort, I opened up my home as our first meeting spot. I lived in a pristine carriage house on a gorgeous gated estate with a mansion just steps from my door. My beloved friends lived in the main house, so inviting people over always felt safe, as there were plenty of people around.

"Let's not try to meet at the restaurant. There's no way to judge what time you'll actually be in Sonoma. I don't want you to have the pressure of being on time for this date. Come pick me up, and whenever you arrive is when our date starts."

Sure enough—with traffic, rain, getting lost, and pulling over to text for clarification along the way, he arrived at 8:00 PM, completely frazzled and soaked.

"I took a wrong turn, and the roads are so dark, and there are no lit street signs anywhere."

One look at him and I knew that if we went right back out, his frazzled commute energy would immediately clash with his priority to produce a satisfactory date for the both of us—getting us to the restaurant, getting seated, ordering—so I smiled, took his drenched coat, handed him a glass of wine and said, "We're in no hurry. Let's sit down so you can relax from that commute."

As he stepped across my threshold he encountered warm, dim lighting and calming music (Billy Bragg, Cat Power, and the like), uncorked (breathing) red wine and a platter filled with the best cheeses, fruit, olives, and salami in wine country.

We never made it to the restaurant.

~ ~ ~

What I did right: I allowed time for him to arrive, shake off all that rain, and transition from his commute into connecting and hanging out with me, instead of trying to rush him out the door to the hottest restaurant just for the sake of starting a date. I also anticipated his need for food and had snacks ready on arrival. I rock.

So what happened?

We spent time together right up until he relocated to the South to be near his children. I still adore him. He's sexy, a captivating storyteller, and a very cool person.

17

Sorting Your Mate

Who are you looking for?

Tall, dark, and handsome?

Mr. CEO Executive?

Sensitive, creative artist?

Instinct will compel you to pick based on your sexual attraction and level of chemistry. Unfortunately, chemistry and sexual attraction don't always have much to do with lasting compatibility. Said another way, when we put sexual attraction above all else, we end up looking for what's attractive instead of what's important. A date you physically desire may not have anything you need to make you happy for more than two hours, let alone happy for the rest of your life.

In my personal experience and in countless experiences of women I've known and worked with, if you have sexual desire for someone on a scale from one to ten, with ten being strongest desire, the tens are the those with whom you have a tougher chance of being happy with in a long-term relationship. With them you don't have access to your best self. You're all grabby hormones and crazy sauce and not acting anything like who you really are. If you currently have a ten in your life, I bet that right now your instincts are screaming, "Don't listen to buzzkill Wendy; burn her book and keep him!"

Chemistry is just mean. I'll admit I'm usually most affected by a man's height. My favorite height for a man is six-foot-five. My first-ever romantic partner (at the tender age of fifteen) was six feet, five inches tall. Coincidence? No, it's called imprinting. I live in the land of the five-foot-seven-inch man, and it left me kinda out of luck, but that's not a terrible thing. Why? Because six-foot-five has nothing to do with the qualities in a man that make me ridiculously happy and everything to do with what my hindbrain lusts after.

Now, I'm not telling you *not* to date tall men. Most of us have a reasonably strong preference that our guys be taller than we are. It's far from a necessity, but I'd be lying if I said it wasn't a thing—for me, anyway.

I dated one man who was six-foot-six. He turned out to be mean and not particularly bright and to have opposing values to mine. And, yes, he was handsome. When I looked up at him, my body wanted to respond like a magnet, pulling my frame straight toward his chest. But that lusty desire has nothing to do with us being compatible partners for each other. I knew for sure I'd never be my favorite self with him, no matter how tall or hot he was.

Think of a man from your past—a ten on the scale. What if you had to spend the rest of your life with him? In a Laundromat, at the grocery store, the home improvement store on a Sunday afternoon, doing house and yard chores together, making the family budget, and filing taxes. Would you be happy? Or would you just want to hang yourself? Alas, most of our life is not spent between 1,000-thread-count Egyptian cotton sheets in a villa in the Caribbean.

Our instinctual demands usually translate to the desire for these sorts of things in a man:

- Height (at least four inches taller than you)[4]

- Resources (money, property, connections)
- Status (think politicians, rock stars, high-level executives)
- Strength (both mental and physical: muscles, smarts, humor)
- Beauty (excellent genes for your children, whether you want children or not)

While the above list is by no means true for everyone, you need look no further for its widespread relevance than at a man's online profile page on almost any online dating company site. Just look to the side for fixed pull-down bars and check boxes for age, height, income, job, and let's not forget the all-important photos that show us his physical attractiveness.

Instinct does this to us because it wants us to survive. Instinct still thinks we need big, strong men to take care of us. "Big, strong man" these days translates to things like status, looks, and education—the modern-day equivalents of having most of his teeth and broad shoulders to throw you over on your way back to the most rockin' cave in the clan. But instinct, while effective at keeping the human race alive, can be, well, kind of gross when it comes to finding our partner.

In the past, I bet you've made a list—if not on paper then a mental one of the qualities you're looking for in your husband or mate. Actually, it wasn't you making the list; the "who" drafting it was instinct. It might look something like this:

- Six feet tall (height)
- Dark hair, beautiful eyes, above-average good looks (beauty)
- Charming and charismatic with excellent social skills (status)
- Educated at a university (strength and status)

I've just described Ted Bundy, one of America's most notorious criminals, a serial killer, rapist, kidnapper, and necrophile. Yikes.

Or

- Six-foot-four (height)
- Mega-rich (resources)
- Knows every-damned-body in Hollywood (resources)
- Can get us into any club, anytime (status)
- Smart and funny (strength)

I've just described Snoop Dogg. (I have a thing for Snoop.) Or one inch taller? Howard Stern.

No, I am not comparing Snoop and Howard to Ted. What I'm highlighting here is that these qualities alone do not get you what will make you happy. Besides that, Snoop and Howard are taken. Ladies, you do not want a celebrity wife coming after you.

I recommend torching that old list of yours because you're about to make a new list, and in doing so you're going to work out who it is you're really looking for (and his eye color will make no difference). Let's call the list you're about to make your "unicorn" list, considering that there's probably no person on the planet who encompasses everything on it. But don't worry; we're going to start with the unicorn list and then we're going to run it through a sieve to see what your minimum requirements are. In doing this, we're going to discover not just what you want but also what you need.

Ready?

Your Unicorn List

Make your unicorn list of things you're upset, off-balance, or unwell without. Going without them is too cruel to bear. These are things you need. Examples might include "loves my body as it is; we have sex at least twice a month; often sees me as interesting and funny; is willing to take me to the ballet once a year; appreciates my talent of cooking."

Then make a list of qualities, traits, physical descriptions, habits, and abilities that are important to you and that a mate should already possess before he meets you. Examples could include "kind, playful, loving, generous, fun, chivalrous, responsible for his own happiness, passionate, a life lover, an adventurer, family-oriented, respectful to everyone (especially people on the front lines of the service industry), strong sense of self, tolerant and inclusive of diversity and minorities, politically and spiritually compatible."

Next, add qualities your most beloved friends have that you admire and appreciate. Examples: "Decisive, whip-smart, irreverent, funny, moderate in vices, authentic, allows for my self-expression, is a wordsmith."

Finally, add qualities you love that you possess. Examples: "optimistic, clean, generous, safe."

Take a look back at what you've just written. You've got a lot on this page, yes? You may even have more than one page. That's fine; this is your unicorn list. Let it run free. You can have everything, including the kitchen sink, on it because we're about to do some thinning. One quality at a time, we're going to run this list through your filter of minimum requirements.

Your Filtered List

Take the first quality at the top of your unicorn list and ask yourself this question: "Would I rather be alone than with someone who isn't _____?"

This is a stand-alone evaluation; each item on the list should be evaluated against being alone. Start from the first quality, and if you'd rather be alone than be without it, keep it. If there's wiggle room, scratch it off the list and move to the next quality until you go all the way through your list.

What Contradicts on Your List?

Take a gander at your list and see if there are certain traits that contradict other traits on your list or don't mesh with them. For example, "type A, highly driven, and financially successful" are qualities that may make your list, but "dedicated to spending a lot of time with me" and "makes family a top priority" might also be on your list. 411: all these qualities in one person can only be found in Hollywood movies. In the real world these are two separate people, not one person. Reevaluate your list to see if one trait contradicts another.

Once you've edited your list, write the following questions:

- How does he make me feel safe?
- How does he make me feel empowered?
- How does he allow for my self-expression?
- How does he comfort me?
- How does he show me I'm beautiful?

Is he adoring of you? What does that look like to you? Does he take charge and save you from the spider in the bathtub? How does he show he cares? And is it in the currency you need?

Also important to add to your list are any deal-breakers. Examples: "smoker, has young children, heavy drinker . . . serial killer."

Narrow It Down Even More

After you've completed your unicorn list, go back and pare the qualities down to your top eight. Memorize these eight musts so when someone says, "What are you looking for?" you're not rolling your eyes back into your head trying to remember your nine-page list. You'll be able to rattle off the top eight in one cohesive statement:

"I'm looking for a man who's a lot like me—he's kind of a smarty-pants. He's an irreverent wordsmith who's decisive, kind, and chivalrous. Oh, and he loves having a lot of sex with me."

Boom. There it is.

This list grounds you in who you are, what you're looking for, and what your life could be like. Having that kind of clarity makes a big difference in the sorting process. It's like having your wardrobe colors done. I did that. Now that I know what my colors are (and which ones they are not), I can walk into a store and look past those in-fashion bright yellow or lime-green jackets and say, "Nope," and walk right out. They aren't in my color palette. I'm not wasting my time.

Know who you are. Know what you want. And at the end of the day, file these lists somewhere you can reference them for when you meet someone you're all hopped-up on chemistry for and you need a reality check.

Use them as a guide, not as hard-and-fast rules. Be willing to let God, the Universe, karma, serendipity, Spirit, Allah, Buddha— whoever or whatever—surprise you. Don't be too rigid if an amazing person shows up who doesn't have everything on your list. If you are your favorite self with that person, then give him a chance (excluding your deal-breakers, of course).

This is key information that needs to live in your filing cabinet. Rather than whip these details out on a first date, use them when writing your online dating profile instead so daters can sort themselves out prior to meeting you at your favorite coffee shop.

Navigating Your Differences

The two of you will be different. Sometimes opposites attract; instinct has a hand in that. For the areas where you're different or even opposite, you will need to see if you can align those differences or work with them. Some things you can align on; others you'll need to make deals to have what you both need. Then there are some that just turn into deal-breakers. This depends on the two of you and your unique points of view. You could have the exact challenges as another couple, and you two might work it out while others just couldn't do it.

For example: You're an early riser who wakes up at 5:00 AM and he's a late sleeper who wakes up at 11:00 AM. This could be a problem. For some it's a deal-breaker. For others it's a welcome difference and they take advantage of the blocks of "alone time." If you're willing to make differences workable for everyone, first, you need to be honest about what you need. Second, you need to be as cool with it as he is with you so that neither of you are invalidating each other or trying to change the other from who they are or what they need.

Are you an introvert? Can you be with an extrovert? Are you a social butterfly but your date is socially awkward and seriously shy? I leave this up to you two to work out. Sometimes social butterflies and painfully awkward individuals work well together and it's sweet.

Are you laid-back or intense? Sometimes it's better to ask your friends these questions. I once described myself as laid-back to Seattle Nate, and he laughed so hard he cried. Sometimes we don't see ourselves clearly. And sometimes one person's easygoing is another one's high-maintenance. It's all about how you relate to and meld with each other.

Listen and Learn

Listen up, ladies. Most of us know by now that the interview (or, as I like to refer to it, the interrogation) process for dating is out, so how are you going to extract the information you need to get to know the guy? I'm going to show you what to do to obtain quality information from men—without the interrogation. This process is easy but I'll warn you it's also counterintuitive and awkward.

When you arrive on a date, use the "know him" technique described earlier: All you do is ask a simple question like, "How was your day?" Then do two things.

One: listen to what he says. If you want him to really open up, you may need a new way to listen. Listening looks like this:

> Just listen.
> Don't interrupt.
> Don't even nod your head while he's talking.
> Don't ask more questions.
> Just. Listen.

Are you ready for the hardest part? After he stops talking, keep listening (not talking) for twenty-five seconds longer.

That's right; twenty-five whole seconds. This is not normal. Right now, I double-dog dare you to experiment with this. Grab your watch or smartphone and time yourself for twenty-five seconds. Pretend you're being silent in front of your date this long. I bet you'll be squirming out of your seat after five seconds. I know I was the first (or fourth or fifth) time I tried this.

But if you allow that twenty-five seconds of space to exist, most often he'll have something more to say because it can take eighteen to twenty-three seconds for most men to respond and say more. If you wait you will often hear something deeper than what he started with.

Good, yes?

I'm glad you think it's good because here comes an even harder part. When he stops talking, wait another twenty-five seconds (rinse and repeat). Again, usually, women don't wait. We keep going and going and going. But if you try this, he will tell you everything you ever needed to know and more without your having to grill him for information like a cop going at a suspect.

Okay, here's part two: listen to what he has to say like you're trying to learn something new about him. Well, duh, right? But here's the thing: when we listen, there's a filter that gets in the way of us really listening to people in order to learn something. When you're listening to someone sharing their opinion about anything, your brain immediately tries to figure out whether you agree or disagree.

Go ahead and try it out in the next conversation you have. Seriously, I bet you'll hear your brain firing up and asking, "Do I agree or do I disagree?" as soon as the other person starts talking.

This question is the thing that is often in the way of you getting the information you need, and it messes with your sorting process too.

You might think the agree or disagree question would give you all the information and would be useful if you actually agree. But trust me, it's an information blocker. So instead of posing that internal question, consciously listen to him to learn something new. In this instance conscious listening might look like:

- Who is this person?
- What does he value?
- What's important to him?
- What's he passionate about?
- What about this topic makes it a top priority for him?
- Wow—why is he starting the conversation here?

This makes acquiring the information you need possible without the aid (or crutch) of your dating checklist. As an added bonus, this technique makes men think you have mad listening skills (and really, you do).

Try this as well: instead of asking yourself "Is he . . . ?" or "Isn't he . . . ?" shift to "How is he . . . ?" For example: "How is he generous?" instead of, "Is he generous?" This shifts the question from a simple yes or no answer to a more open-ended and informative response. By doing these things, you'll learn more of what you need to see if you two stand a chance.

These listening techniques are exercises created by Alison Armstrong (she uses thirty seconds, actually). I've taught them to thousands (yes, thousands) of women in a workshop I lead through PAX Programs, and I have yet to meet the woman who didn't experience the "Do I agree or disagree?" phenomenon. And when we listen twenty-five seconds longer, miracles happen. I offer it up as homework to my participants on the first night of the workshop, and consistently, women come back the next morning bursting to share the gems men provided when they were given the space to talk. The staff at PAX Programs (including me) have spent the last twenty-plus years conducting social research on this by waiting to see how long it takes men to respond and asking men how much time they'd like to respond, and what we found is it takes anywhere between eight to twenty-three seconds for a man to formulate what he's going to say next. We women rarely wait past a few seconds. Without the gap, most men don't speak.

Dave and I were at an event where we were asked to sit in groups of four. Our group comprised three women and Dave. When it was his turn to talk, the two other women looked at him, waited about two seconds, and started talking over his turn. He never spoke. (I watched in amusement—you know I like a good science experiment.) When we got home and I asked him about it, he said, "I knew what I wanted to contribute, but I will only speak into five seconds of silence."

How many seconds of silence do you allow for?

Who's My Mate?

You've done the work to know who you are, who you're looking for, and what your life could look like, and you've learned new listening skills to get the information you need. As you start to look, I encourage you to be willing to look outside your type. You know what your "type" has gotten you in the past. Is the man who's asking you out handsome but he doesn't look like the guys you usually date? Good. Maybe his profile seems interesting but you've never dated this flavor of man before. Excellent. You might consider giving him a try.

As I said earlier, after dating 121 men, I learned I can date outside my type but I can't date outside my "tribe." For me, there has to be shared or complementary ways of seeing the world for things to work out. We need to have resonance and common ground. I need to feel I have a sense of where he's coming from and that he sees and knows me. That creates the opportunity for mutual respect. Does this mean we have to be like-minded on every important thing? Nope.

Dave and I love music. He's a fantastic piano and keyboard player, talented enough to be in bands on the really big stages, and at one point he did about a hundred gigs in one year as his passion hobby job. We have opposite tastes in music. He values complexity while I value simplicity. He values rhythm while I value lyrics. The genres of music we like are unrelated. Together we've taught one another a broader sense of music and can respect (and enjoy) where the other is coming from. And ultimately our love of music is something we have in common.

Say yes to the ones you find interesting. Say yes to the ones you think you might admire or respect once you get to know them.

Giving someone a chance allows him the opportunity to grow on us. Not all will, of course, but a good match just might. Our culture feeds us fairy tales like "happily ever after," "meant to be," "love at first sight," and "The One," and we buy them. The narrative we're all too familiar with usually goes like this: If we don't fall in love instantly, then it's not meant to be because he's not "The One." That's crap. What if he is your guy and he's amazing for you but he was sick on your first date? Or he was so nervous he didn't show his true

personality well? Because you didn't see stars in the first twenty minutes, are you going to chuck this one back?

Now, here's where it gets tricky—finding a balance between
protecting your precious time and giving a date a chance. I'm often
asked, "How long do I give him a chance to grow on me?" This is a
complex question, and there are four parts to the answer:

1. Sort for the things you need in a partner (as above).
2. Use your instincts. (Your gut knows.)
3. Date him for a while and see if you really like this person.
   Can you envision the two of you having enough material to
   cover you through three days of being trapped in a public
   Laundromat, for example? Anyone can have fun for three
   nights in Paris, but do you think you could do dull everyday stuff with him for three days in a row (laundry, grocery
   shopping, cleaning your house) and still like him? Really
   like him? Use the Laundromat test.
4. Don't hang out because he likes you too much. Here's a trap
   that can happen: You want to give him a chance to grow on
   you. He's a nice guy. So you date him. It's okay. You're kinda
   bored but you're hoping it gets better, so you keep dating
   him. And he treats you so well. No man has ever treated you
   this well before. All your girlfriends are saying he's an amazing prospect and how you should keep dating him. Now
   you feel pressure. Pressure from your girlfriends, pressure
   because you don't want to be displeasing to him because he's
   really attracted to you and he's amazing, but you know in
   your gut you're never going to be happy with this guy. It's a
   common scenario. I know a woman who was in this situation and stayed long enough to have two kids and a ten-year
   marriage. Don't be her. If your date is not the right match for
   you, don't stay. It's not fair to anyone.

Once you know who you are and can distinguish type from tribe, you can quickly sort through the dates who are clearly not a match because you're not on the same page.

Date #52
Opposites Don't Always Attract

Setting: Coffee Shop, Mill Valley, CA

He was late—really late. This popular chain coffee shop is not the best spot for intentionally childless adults like me. It had been transformed into a daycare center for toddlers screaming and running up and down the rows, colliding into strangers' chairs like bumper cars. When I grew up, coffee was an adult beverage. I could have sworn we childless peeps had dibs on coffee shops and bars and parents had dibs on, well, everything else. But I digress. Between the wildly expressive tots and gaggles of giggling teenagers, I felt entirely middle-aged and curmudgeonly.

Finally, Date #52 arrived, and he looked, um . . . interesting. I couldn't tell if he was trying to be intentionally retro-hip and just missed the mark a little bit or if he was just some random suburban guy who had his own thing going on stylewise. He was a schoolteacher who hated to travel, loved to be around small children, didn't like pets, felt work was the most important thing in his life, and spent all his spare time on DIY projects around his suburban home. In other words, he was the polar opposite of me.

"Can we make a plan for next weekend?" he asked. *Oh, God, no,* I thought. Didn't I point out how mismatched we were?

"Thank you for asking, but I don't think we're quite a match," I replied. He began the protest with, "You're not even going to give us a chance . . ."

I interrupted: "Look, our lives are almost completely opposite. I'm sorry, but everything that holds your interest just doesn't hold mine. And the things that are important to me aren't what you value."

He protested but could see I was nearing the end of my iced tea and I wasn't going to budge on this one.

- Make your list. Know your list. But don't grill your dates with your list.
- Really listen. See where it takes you and what it shows you.
- Understand the difference between type and tribe. Give him a chance to grow on you, but don't be afraid to say no when you know he's not your mate.

18

The Divorced Guy (Best-Kept Secret or Total Nightmare?)

My experiences and the experiences of many a friend and client have taught me a lot about recently divorced, long-divorced, and soon-to-be divorced men. A man coming out of a painful divorce (whether it's his first or his eighth) will be very happy to have your company. He'll enjoy spending time with you because being out with a woman who's interested in spending time with him is going to make him feel amazing and he probably hasn't felt anywhere close to that in a while.

He will also probably have little to no interest in giving you anything lasting—or even have the ability to do so.

You want to think of it like this: When he met you, he was in a deep, dark hole. And you, my friend, are the ladder he uses to climb out of that hole. Once he climbs all the way out, it probably won't occur to him to take the ladder with him. He'll step out, see the sunshine, and say, "Wow, life is beautiful. Look over there." And he'll be gone. This is what some of us refer to as a rebound.

This doesn't happen with every man in every divorce. A rebound situation tends to happen when a man is having a particularly painful divorce (often an unexpected first). Some men rebound with a woman for a few months; others rebound with a woman and stay with her for a year or so but are ultimately unable to commit to her; and then again, some men couple up and can happily commit despite the long-past, recent, or pending divorce.

In case you find yourself reading this to try to diagnose which kind of divorced man you have on your hands because you don't want to invest your whole heart on someone who will be gone in a couple months, understand this: there are always exceptions. Don't turn away a worthy man just because he's recently divorced. If you're willing, hang out for a bit to see how he's relating to you. Did he seek you out? If you reached out to him, that's still okay. Is he initiating contact and is he the one planning dates?

Whether or not he was the one who initiated the divorce might be a factor. If it was a total surprise to him, he might be at the bottom of that hole, whereas if he was the one who asked for the divorce or it was a long-overdue mutual decision, he may have been processing the completion of that relationship for months, years, or even decades while he was in it—and prior to meeting you.

If you're seeing a man who is in a hole and you know you're his potential ladder but you want to keep dating him anyway, go for it. Just don't con yourself. Use the experience for good and for your pleasure without trying to turn it into something serious.

I've heard women say, "You don't want a divorced guy; he's used," or I've heard them referred to as someone else's leftovers. This is ridiculous. I think divorced guys are awesome because:

- Many of them know how to and are (eventually) willing to commit.
- They made mistakes in their marriage and (hopefully) learned from them.
- They watched their ex-wife make mistakes and can save you from making the same ones.

- Throughout (or after) their marriage, they gained realistic expectations of what partnership is. A man who has never been married is making up what his future should look like based on the fantasies and fairy tales our culture feeds us.

- If he has children, you have the added bonus of having a man who has had his illusions shattered in the best of ways. Chances are he knows how to roll with anything. A dad has had tiny people vomit on him in the middle of the night and he loves them anyway. Now, that's staying power.

May I add for the record that Dave was newly separated when we met? He had only been separated from his wife of twenty-four years for a few months. I was his first date in decades. By all accounts, this pairing should not have worked, except it did. We are ridiculously well matched for each other.

When it comes to dating the newly divorced man, here are more things to consider: When you're first starting to date, don't ask him what happened in his marriage. He just might tell you, and before you know it, you're playing the role of therapist, listening to his four-and-a-half-hour story. It's not sexy to you or to him, and it may end the connection right there.

Also, it's best to leave money out of the conversation—at least at first. His whole financial world could have shifted and he may need some time to adjust and rethink how he lives his life and spends his money. On more than one occasion I was triggered into wondering if he was cheap when that wasn't the case at all; it was a calibration issue that corrected in time. And whatever the story is between him and his ex, do not—I repeat, *do not*—interfere with his money and the money he pays her. This is not your business, my friend, even if you wind up marrying him.

Think of it this way: she was with him, took care of him in her own way, gave him what he needed, and dealt with the much younger, more immature versions of him that you never had to see. For example, I know I got Dave 4.0 (the latest and greatest model), and his ex-wife got the previous versions all the way back to Dave 1.0, which, according to him, was no picnic. Consider that your sweetheart's ex might have earned every penny. Whether it's true or not, it will help you sleep through the night and be a nicer person on the planet.

So you have been dating this sweet divorced guy for a while now, and you are starting to wonder, "How do I get him to commit to me?"

Sister, you don't. If you've been single for a while and he's the newly divorced guy—and you're not the ladder—then I suggest you let him lead. I told Dave shortly after we started dating that I was looking for my partner. I didn't need to be married—I'd done that before—but I did want a lifetime partner, and I wanted him to know that up front. I knew we were in different places, and because he was fresh out of a relationship, I was going to let him set the pace for ours. I was going to let him lead and I would follow. If at any point he saw that we were not a long-term match, then he was to tell me immediately so we could stop dating. Well, he grabbed my hand and started leading us right into our long-term committed relationship.

Dave was the newly divorced guy with the outcome I was looking for. Here's one that didn't go quite so well. Welcome to my own hole-and-ladder experience.

Date #60
I Was the Ladder
(aka Bubble Boy)

Setting: Dinner at Amber India; hiking the steps of Coit
Tower; late-night dessert at Fog City Diner,
San Francisco, CA

He was a slightly more out-there male version of me. Same vernacu-
lar, same point of view. It added a certain creepiness to an otherwise
excellent first date. Our differences came from our upbringing: he, an
only child with a wide well-cushioned net and an ability to do what he
wanted without concern or repercussions; me, not so much. I got my
start as an accessory to a single teenage mother who skillfully navi-
gated her way up the ranks to the middle class. Basically, I'm scrappy.

Within the first ten minutes of our date I suspected he was
not my man, but by this time we'd already ordered food. Halfway
through our dinner he asked, "Ever climbed to the top of Coit Tower
through the private gardens?"

"Nope."

"Want to?"

"Sure."

At the base of Coit Tower, I swapped out my stilettos for the
tennis shoes I had stashed in the trunk of my car (for this very
purpose). We hiked the stairs, admired the view of the Bay and
San Francisco hillside, smelled the roses, peered into rich people's
houses, and enjoyed conversation all the way to the top. And at the
end of such a strenuous, healthy hike, what could be better than
dark molten-chocolate cake, ice cream, and house-made marshmal-
lows at Fog City Diner? Nothing. But the real marshmallow icing
on the cake was that my date is a VIP customer. He called ahead to
reserve his booth, and when we arrived, close to 11:30 PM, it was set
and waiting. As I slid in, I saw golden engraved plaques lining the
wall—legendary *San Francisco Chronicle* columnist Herb Caen and
Charles Williams (founder of Williams-Sonoma)—and then I spotted his name. My date was among the celebrated luminaries. Wow.

"Can I take a picture of you and the plaque on my iPhone?" I asked, half joking, half not.

"No," he kindly declined.

On conclusion, the date was enjoyable, he was a fun guy, and it wasn't a total waste of my Friday night.

So what happened?

By 3:00 AM at the end of our third date, we found ourselves in my car, idling in front of a parking garage. We'd been parked and talking for hours. We didn't want to leave each other's side. This is when we went into "the bubble." I'd never been in a love bubble before. It was elating, that frenzied level of mutual infatuation so strong we knew not to even attempt trying to be around others—we were too goofy.

When a bubble like this pops, it pops from about a thousand feet in the air and someone is dumped out of it on her head (ouch). This was my "newly divorced guy" lesson: Two months into the relationship the bubble burst. He woke up one morning and just didn't feel like being in a relationship with me. Didn't want me gone; just wanted to be dating me along with others. It took me more than two years to get over him.

1. Always have a pair of tennis shoes in your trunk, just in case.
2. Be open to an adventurous time if fun is already being had. Just because the two of you aren't MTB doesn't mean the date has to end early. What else are you going to do with the rest of your Friday night?
3. Enjoy the bubble—newly divorced or no—but tread carefully because bubbles pop.

19

Bringing Out His Confidence

There's something that happens for both men and women on dates: nerves. Men are often nervous on a date just like we are—especially the first date, and even more so if they're attracted to you.

When a man is too attracted to a woman, the same thing happens as when a woman is too attracted to a man. He's trying to impress you but he's nervous, so it is with an "overly pleasing" and "trying too hard" energy, which is often annoying and a turn-off. Now, wouldn't it be a sad loss if you two couldn't connect because of this, even though he is fantastic? Not liking someone because they like you too much is a tragedy.

If he's nervous and you're not sure you're attracted because he's doing that annoying thing you've seen yourself do a hundred times, hang in there—because you've seen glimpses and glimmers of your attraction to him but it keeps going away because you're not seeing his confidence.

When a man is nervous, his confidence—one of the things that makes him sexy to you—is eclipsed behind this too-pleasing behavior spurred on by nerves. You'll need to draw out his confidence, bit by bit. Here's how: the fastest way to access a man's natural confidence is by asking him to talk about his accomplishments, something he's proud of, or his status.

When I say something he's proud of, I don't mean his kids. That's not him. If he keeps shifting to his kids and talking about them, keep moving the conversation back to him as a person. A soft way to do this is by asking what makes him a good father or what lesson he has learned along the way or who his influences are and why.

Here are some possible topics you may hear about when it comes to his pride:

- Work projects, investments, and accomplishments
- His sports
- His writing
- Musical instruments he's learned to play
- Other hobbies he's proficient in and passionate about

The topics themselves may not always be riveting to you, but this approach will get you what you need: he'll be more relaxed, in his element, and—yep—confident. Think about how you must look and act when you're talking about the things you love—sitting up straighter than usual, maybe gesticulating with your hands, smiling, and laughing. This is the you that you want him to see and this is the him you want to see, too. You can bring all this out in him by simply leading him to the topics he wins at regularly, whatever those topics may be for him.

20

Look for "That Look"

One of the things I looked for in a man while on my 121 exploits was how much he liked me. If I were still a teenager, I probably would have asked myself, "How much does he *like* like me?" When I met my match, I expected we'd be compatible in a variety of areas, but one area that's absolutely crucial is the physical. I know I'm smart. I always picked men who saw the intelligence in me; I didn't have to worry about that. But I also needed to know he thought I was beautiful. If a man didn't give me "that look" within the first few dates (you know the one—like he's starving and you're the tastiest snack he's ever seen), I didn't continue dating him. Every exception I made to that rule ended in heartbreak.

When a man thinks that you and your body are beautiful and he expresses his adoration for you and your body, it's heaven on earth and totally worth waiting for. I want that for you.

If you're a person who doesn't need that, one thing to notice on a date is how you are feeling. Are you feeling pretty? Are you feeling funny? Are you feeling known? Are you your best self with him? If you're not feeling it, consider moving along (even if he's the spitting image of Hugh Laurie).

In all my years of doing what I do, one thing still stands out loud and clear: I think that what we really want is to feel like the prize, not that we won the prize. So if you find you're working too hard to convince him you're amazing and he's not picking up what you're throwing down, take a breath and realize that he might not be the guy for you. Or when you catch yourself trying too hard mid-date, simply stop. Stop talking, sit back, and let him generate. When you're over-generating, you're covering both parts—his and yours. As I've mentioned, you're doing all the heavy lifting, and it's exhausting. Give him an opening to pick up where you leave off.

What happens if he doesn't pick up where you left off? Well, that date ends faster, which is actually awesome. You're now freed up to go home and watch HGTV reruns or finish that scrapbooking project that's been collecting dust. How do you think this book got written?

Ultimately I created my own rule: No matter how steamy he is, if he doesn't think I'm hot, he's no longer hot to me.

Here's a man I was crazy about. We clicked so well that I made an exception to my rule. And while I dated him I never felt beautiful, special, or desired—not even for a second. It was a very long five months. Ouch.

Date #113
Off Balance

Setting: Dinner at À Côté, Oakland, CA

My first face-to-face meeting with Date #113 was at À Côté, an intimate Oakland restaurant known to locals as a date spot. He arrived before I did. I spotted him leaning against the restaurant's open door. He smiled, indicating, "It's me."

A week prior, we were both away from California—me in New Orleans, him in Portland. For those six days, we emailed multiple times a day, revealing ourselves and updating each other on the adventures unfolding before us.

Knowing the strong odds against a connection outside of the interweb, I spent that week carefully untangling the strings of connection, anticipation, and hope. I'd done a thorough job partly by trying to trick myself into forgetting what I liked about him. When we met I had few expectations.

The location was my suggestion, and I took the lead with the reservation, requesting a quiet table. The host kindly obliged with a small table for two tucked all the way in the back garden. We slid in, and a battle of wits and playful banter ensued. It was one of those magical nights that all daters hope for. Seamless flow of conversation, genuine interest from both sides (or so I hoped), and a mutual appreciation of each other's wit, sincerity, and knowledge.

He sat back after his meal, seemingly nowhere near ready to leave, and his salt-and-pepper hair fell to the left side. As he swept it back, he pulled both hands behind his head and leisurely leaned back, and it hit me: I was seriously crushing on him—he's sexy. He'd already won me over with his personality, but I was suddenly taken by how handsome he was, and he had a style I like: jeans and a sweater—casual, simple, understated, solid. No weird patterns or suburban golf shirt, no outlandish tennis shoes; in fact, nothing he wore even resembled the color tan.

Several hours and dozens upon dozens of stories in, I could see that even though we had been among the first to arrive, we were now the very last to leave. I didn't want to go anywhere. I didn't want to move. I wanted to revel in the fact that this whole dating thing might actually be working.

As we left the restaurant, he walked me to my car, and the moment I stopped on the driver's side, he leaped over to the curb by the passenger side, about seven feet from me. The speed at which he moved and the large gap between us caught me by complete surprise. *Wow—he really doesn't want to kiss me; he moved away from me ridiculously fast. Oh . . . oh, crap. He doesn't want to see me again. How could I miss this?* As these thoughts swirled around my head, through the noise I heard him say, "So should we do this again?"

"Yes!" I exclaimed.

He shifted and his eyes rolled back a little.

"No?" I asked in a soft, almost pleading whine of a voice.

"Yes. I'm just thinking about my schedule. Today is Monday; maybe this Saturday. I have to double-check."

Breathe, Wendy, breathe.

So what happened?

I used to run around telling my girlfriends I was looking for tall, clever, and British. This date taught me that what I was really looking for was a like-minded wordsmith who's irreverent, decisive, and chivalrous. Throw in sexual compatibility and the appropriate dose of adoration and I would have been all his.

I had high hopes for this one. He was amazing and truly a good guy who meant no harm, but the key element missing was adoration. I didn't see that he had any for me. We had regular dinner dates (and nothing more) before I learned he'd decided around our third date that we had no future—but I was "fun" and he enjoyed my company, so he kept asking me out. And there I sat, several months later in the middle of an Ethiopian jazz bar, completely heartbroken, trying not to cry in front of him, and praying for the check to come as I toiled at the end of the string he'd (unintentionally) been dangling all along.

Like I said: ouch.

Hot Tip Remember that list you made a while ago? The one you distilled down from your unicorn list of musts that your partner absolutely has to have no matter what? I'll say it a million times and it'll still be just as true: don't compromise on it. Don't keep dating someone if you're getting less than what you need.

21

He Never Promised You a Rose Garden

You're on a date. You like where this is going. He's funny, he's cute, he's asking you about your life, he's telling you about his, and you see no red flags (not even a pink Post-it note). Yay!

A couple of hours in, he talks about how every year he spends Christmas at his aunt's house in Lake Tahoe. Oh, yeah, the whole family goes up; it's a big deal. The place has five bedrooms and there's always plenty of room; there's a hot tub; you can ski in and out of the property; and they own a bunch of snowmobiles and everything. Then he says, "Do you even like snowmobiling? My mom and aunt would like you."

It's your first date. It's August. Did he just invite you to Christmas?

Fast-forward to your second date. You discover you both love Elvis Costello. You tell him your favorite song is "Blue Chair" but no one ever knows that one. Your second favorite is "Shipbuilding." He doesn't have a favorite, but he likes yours. Then he says, "I've never known a bigger Elvis fan than me. It would be so fun to see Elvis with you."

Is Elvis even playing in your town soon? Is he asking you to see Elvis Costello with him?

It's your third date. You learn he not only surfs but he spent a summer teaching children how to surf. You know how to boogie board; that's it. You express your love of boogie boarding, and he says, "Oh, that sounds fun, but there's nothing like surfing. Surfing and boogie boarding are different. And you seem athletic; I'm sure you have the core for it. You'd be a natural. I think it would be fun teaching you."

Did he just promise to teach you how to surf? When are you going? Where will you learn? Will you stay overnight? Is he talking about a romantic weekend away in Carmel?

Nope. I'm sorry, my love, but he wasn't. He did not invite you to Christmas or to see Elvis Costello or to spend a romantic weekend in Carmel.

Men do this thing and they don't even know they do it. Alison Armstrong calls it Photoshopping.

He's in front of you but he's picturing you in all kinds of scenarios in his life to see if you'll fit. He's "Photoshopping" you into these scenarios. The problem is, they do this unconsciously and (unfortunately for you) out loud. They have no idea how tempting and easy it is to listen to what they're saying and take it as plans and promises of a future together.

Remember back when you were a little girl and you had a paper doll? The paper doll had paper outfits you could try on her. Maybe a chef's hat or a policewoman's uniform or a nurse's uniform or a skirt and briefcase. Imagine he's trying you on in his life like you tried different outfits on your paper doll. He's trying to see you fit in his world. It's how he can seem like he's coming on too strong. Or how you could seem to come on too strong with him when he's making these comments out loud and you're running with them as a plan.

It's unfair and kind of rage-inducing, and I'm sorry. They don't do it on purpose. They don't do it to hurt us. But know this: if the invitation doesn't have an exact location and a date attached to it, it's not real. I'd say wait for a phrase that sounds something like this: "Would you like to go see Elvis Costello with me at the Great American Music Hall in San Francisco on September third?"

That's how you know it's a plan or a promise.

Instead of getting frustrated with him or overexcited and coming on too strong when he's playing paper dolls with you, you can think instead, "Oh, good, he's seeing how well we fit together, so he most likely likes me," and leave it at that.

Want an example of extreme Photoshopping? Do I have one for you.

Date #73
I'm All Packed,
So Take Me with You

Setting: Oakland airport baggage claim, Oakland, CA

Date #73 was managing the 1 percent, each of whom worked for his daddy. He was hoping for a partner who could travel with him internationally so he'd have a sense of home, since he bounced from a merger to a re-org to a new acquisition. This was his life. Hmm, I wonder who would be a stellar partner for that kind of lifestyle.

His primary residence was in Connecticut, but for business reasons he was looking at a Northern California home to add to the collection.

We'd emailed each other for some time as our travel schedules were off. When we last corresponded, he'd arrived in my area as I was leaving to lead a workshop in Seattle.

I composed a lengthy and revealing email to him on my last night in Seattle. I shared with him my sadness over the recent death of my Husky dog, Eloise, and how traveling the following morning would be brutal, since that was the time I would normally be gearing up to go home to her. I also expressed disappointment that we hadn't met the week before—we had been in the same airport at the same time. I wrapped it up with hope, expressing that I looked forward to meeting him whenever he was back in California.

Early the next morning, as I left the Seattle Renaissance in the drizzly rain, I fought back tears of longing for Eloise. As I slid into the town car to go to the airport, I saw I had my usual driver and he was chatty as always. I did my best to be polite, but I'm certain I fell short. Somehow I managed to hold my composure through airport security, but just as I got in my window seat on the plane, tears started steaming down my face. (I'm not a crier, so this was extremely uncomfortable for me.) Grieving sucks.

Two hours later as the plane landed and taxied, I grabbed the edge of my long skirt to wipe my face and clear away any runny mascara that might be caked under my eyes. I turned on my phone to see if I had any messages. I did. From him.

"I'm so sorry to hear about your dog! I know this is no consolation, and certainly not a replacement, but I've moved my flight to Chicago by a few hours so I could greet you at the airport. I'm in baggage claim waiting for you. Look for me; I'm the tall one." (He's six-foot-five.)

Oh . . . my . . . God. How incredibly sweet, and yet how incredibly horrifying. My eyes were swollen from crying. I had huge bags under them from exhaustion, as I do after leading a workshop for two days. I called him immediately. "Really? You're here?"

"Yes."

"Okay," I said, "there's something you should know. You're seeing me at my worst." I explained about the crying and tiredness as

I made my way to baggage claim. When I arrived, he gave me an enormously strong hug. (I needed that.) And as we were waiting for my bag, I watched the way he looked at me—like a tasty snack, dark circles and runny mascara and all.

We grabbed my luggage, threw it in his car, and drove to a nearby coffee shop, where we chatted for about an hour and a half before he had to head over to a different airport to catch his plane.

This man deserved a medal. On this day, he was my hero.

So what happened?

We spent our second date shopping for his new home. He described his Connecticut estate in great detail, painting pictures of me there in the fall. We daydreamed about our new international travel schedule. My impeccable organizational skills and good company would make each one comfortable. I was in—and I lived each daydream as if it were coming true. A few months of dating revealed that while we seemed perfect on paper (to me, anyway), we were not at all compatible. We seemed to push each other's buttons, and my intentions and words were often misinterpreted.

~ ~ ~

Photoshopping: It's tempting to jump on the bandwagon when the ride looks like a glorious one. I got hooked countless times, even when I knew better. When you catch yourself listening like it's a plan or a promise, remember to look for the date and location. These things can point to the difference between make-believe and real-life plans.

When there's a lot at stake—when you really, really, really like him—we are more susceptible to magical thinking, and that ends up biting us in the ass. It's fine to dream, but remember to stay lightly tethered to the ground.

22

Paying for Dates

"How do I handle myself gracefully when the bill comes?"

My friends, gather around: I have the answer to this age-old question.

Some women expect men to pay; others expect to go dutch. Many of us are experts at the fake-purse grab. Some men want to treat and provide; others just want things to be fair and square between parties. And any man can feel burned out buying a string of meals for strangers he'll never see again.

It can be a conundrum, and there's a lot of unnecessary bullshit surrounding this topic. But it's a topic that's going to come up at some point in your dating experience, so we may as well talk about it now.

Consider that if a man is out to find a compatible long-term partner, he may have to date 100 women. That may sound like a lot but let's face it: I dated 120 men before I found my partner. Seattle Nate believes he's over 200, but he's too exhausted to count, poor guy.

Let's do some basic math: 100 dates, of which 99 percent will not work out in the long term. Let's say the average cost of a date, including food, parking, drinks, and maybe even two tickets to an event, is roughly $100 per date—some more expensive, some less.

That's 100 dates at $100 each, totaling $10,000—just to see if there's a chance of finding your mate.

Now, here's my question to you: Would you want to spend $10,000 of your hard-earned money on the strangers you date? Uh, no, not if you could help it.

A man took a woman I once knew out to a high-end hotel in Beverly Hills. He bought dinner, paid for the entertainment, and drinks. At the end of the date, she was furious that he didn't pay for her valet parking. Similarly, a friend of mine once said, "When a man doesn't offer to pay, he's telling me I'm not special."

I will tell you what I told her: if you weren't the right girl for him, consider that you're not special. I don't mean that you're not special in an objective sense; I mean you're not special to him, and that's okay. This street goes both ways.

To deal with this issue head-on, you want to manage expectations on paying for dates from the beginning. It's totally acceptable to make first meet-and-greets free or inexpensive, and if he offers to pay, be gracious and thank him for the gift of treating you. If you're in that uncomfortable moment when the check comes at the end of dinner (you know, the purse-reach moment) and he's lingering to pick up the bill off the table, instead of the fake-purse grab, you could say, "May I help?"

"May I help?" is the partner question. And it puts the situation squarely back in his lap to either say, "No, I got it," or "Sure, you can pay the tip," or even "Sure, your half is . . ." When you do this, you're being courteous and thoughtful, willing to help and pay if needed but also 100 percent ready to be a gracious receiver.

"But what if that bill just sits there in between us?" you might ask. Well, here are two options: First, wait. Just wait it out. He'll get to it, and as he does, ask, "May I help?" Option two might be used if you're ready to ditch the date or if looking at that thin plastic casing with a receipt hanging out of it is making you so tense you can't talk anymore. You can point to it, nod to it, or reach for it and say, "How would you like to handle this?" and potentially work in some version of "May I help?" based on how he responds.

Say he's paying. You are now obliged to him. Whoa, back up—I don't mean obliged to sleep with him. The obligation I'm talking about is one of thanks. Let's use dinner as an example. You could thank him for any or all of these four things:

- Paying
- The food
- The atmosphere
- The company

It might look something like this:

"David, thank you so much for taking care of dinner for us. My scallops were delicious, and this restaurant is beautiful. I so enjoyed our evening. I think my favorite topic was learning about your dog and her backstory. She sounds adorable."

However you thank him, the most important part is to be authentic. Sincere appreciation is the only exchange most men expect. They may be hopeful for more, but a direct, true show of appreciation is really all it takes to keep the men you date in fine shape too.

And after the first date or two, let him provide if he likes, but partner, you need to find fun ways to pitch in too. Maybe he buys dinner and you pick up the round of drinks afterward. Pack a picnic lunch for a hike. Bring cookies or muffins as an added perk to a quickie coffee date. Show that you have his back and he's not shouldering the load.

Sex Talk on a First Date

A woman once asked me, "When a man talks about sex on the first date, is that inappropriate? Even when he's just speaking in generalities, I still feel uncomfortable. It seems a bit early; we barely know each other."

As a general rule, a man who talks a lot about sex on the first date would like to have sex with you on that first date. It's that simple. He's optimistic. He hopes you pick up what he's laying down. He's sexually attracted to you but there's not enough of a connection (or he's not in the frame of mind for) anything much beyond sex. If there were, he wouldn't risk it. There would be too much to lose in blowing it with you by talking about sex so soon.

Sex is a suitable topic for a first date if you're looking for a hookup. And as you know, I'm the last person to judge you if that's what you're looking for.

If he's talking a lot about sex on the first date, take mental note of it. What he's telling you is he's sexually attracted to you (which is awesome), but he may not be thinking about you for anything more than a night or two. If there's something more for him than just sexual attraction, he won't risk it (unless he's had one too many glasses of red wine—also worthy of noting).

If he brings up sex, test the waters by trying out something like this: "It's way too soon for me to have this conversation. Can we save sex talk for when we know each other better?" Then carefully watch what he says.

Here are two fine examples of overly optimistic suitors. They were sexually attracted and more than slightly misguided.

Date #3
Neato Speedo
(aka The Danish Package)

Setting: His residence, Sonoma, CA

I'm breaking tradition from my first-date stories to give you this second date, as it was far more interesting then our first. Our first date was "fine"; it was dinner.

I agreed to a second date—dinner at his house. Sure, I'd have the chance to get to know him better, but this would also be my sneaky opportunity to see the inside of his Sonoma hills home. I love a canyon home that has deer for neighbors; it makes for tasty daydream material. Some women fantasize about the wedding day; I fantasized about a shared life together.

His midcentury wooden hillside home was well kept and in harmony with the trees surrounding it. My host, smiling at the front door, took me through a modest entrance into a modern kitchen that opened out to a narrow dining room with floor-to-ceiling windows showcasing the forest beyond his decks. Lovely.

We paused in the kitchen. Vegetables on the counter were uncut. There didn't seem to be any food prepped, cooking, thawing, marinating, or cooling.

"I'm sorry dinner isn't under way," he blurted out in response to the look on my face. "I just moved in and I got a little carried away with tidying up the place for you. I had to decide, did I want to cook or clean? And I felt cleaning was more important. I haven't even had time for a shower. Would you mind terribly if I jumped in the shower? After that I'll start cooking dinner right away." He spoke while swiftly moving through the kitchen, setting two clear flute champagne glasses down on the black marble countertop. He picked up a bottle of Gloria Ferrer and twisted the top of a cork clockwise. I set my mind at ease.

Just moved. Fair enough. I could understand that. He handed me a full glass of Gloria and said, "You can wait for me on my deck. Enjoy the view and relax."

"Okay." I was still a bit uneasy but figured I could drink my sparkling wine and whisper for the neighboring deer to come by and keep me company. The outstretched Adirondack-style chaise lounge made for a cozy spot to take in the warmth of the summer evening.

I suppose my mind wandered in the seclusion of the serene space. All at once he was there, standing right next to my chair. All six-foot-two of him, and he was almost naked. A very hairy chest, light hair on his legs, and skimpy Speedo-style underwear in spiral patterns of blues, greens, and yellows.

"You know, Americans are so uptight about the body. They never wear underwear like this."

Oh . . . my . . . God. Is this happening?

"American men are so frumpy. They have no style," he said, leaning in a bit with his eye-level package mere inches from my nose.

"I think you should know one of the reasons I want to date you," he continued, "is because I need to have sex with larger women. I'm so well endowed, I hurt women of normal or smaller size."

Oh holy Jesus. Just start talking, Wendy. You'll figure it out.

"Wow—um, okay, I'm out. Thank you for having me over, but I won't be staying for dinner." I tried to rise to my feet from the opposite side of the lounge chair so I didn't accidentally brush up against his ginormous package of junk wrapped tightly in the Speedo.

"No, no, wait! I'll put on some clothes. We can start dinner right now."

"Nope. That's okay. I can see myself out."

"But I haven't shown you my new Lamborghini!"

I continued to holler back niceties as I moved swiftly out the front door.

Special note: coming to the party like you're about to lose a game of strip poker is never a first-class move unless you have a general consensus that everyone will end up in the same state of nakedness.

Also? Seeing a new Lamborghini does not erase, mitigate, or cancel out inappropriate behavior in any way.

Yeah, don't go to a man's house on the second date.

Truth be told, though, I never did learn that lesson. I'm an optimist. I believe deep down to my core that most men are not like this. Most men would actually like to have their date over for dinner. They may be optimistic for more but wouldn't be so idiotic as to take the Speedo approach.

Date #54
Keeping Up with Mr. Johnson

Setting: Drinks and dinner at Piazza D'Angelo Ristorante, Mill Valley, CA

"I'm sorry. We'll have take it slow. I'm injured," my date said as he hobbled toward me. All hunched over and moving at a painstakingly snail-like speed, he'd inadvertently aged himself. His online profile read forty-eight (which I can say with confidence was untrue) and at first glance, I'd guess him closer to seventy-eight.

He beamed at me confidently, completely unaffected by the state of his wardrobe, which made me question his sanity and state of living conditions—like whether he actually had a roof over his head at night or not. The 1970s were groovy, but the light-tan corduroy jacket needed to be retired after the enormous red wine stain across the lapel had set in (as faded as it was, my guess was several years ago). His T-shirt had lettering on it (I didn't bother to read it) and food stains and grease in swirls and patterns from top to bottom. I tried not to look at his pants.

Since I'm generally agreeable, and because I was already there, I was going to make the best of it. And as many good women do, I had the thought, "If he turns out to be fantastic, I'll dress him."

Our plan was to meet for a drink at the local Italian restaurant in town. After he chose the table, he asked for a menu.

"Wait, we said drinks only, right?" I asked.

"No, I'm hungry. You should order something."

To make a long and boring evening brief and less torturous for you, I'll just say the conversation was tedious. He offered nothing. I had to extract information and encourage his participation by throwing out topics for him to consider like throwing chum to the fishies. At least the fishies bite. This type of nonparticipation is commonly demonstrated by a man who doesn't want to be on a date with you but isn't man enough to end it. With fifty-three dates under my belt, I was well familiar with this scenario. But in this case, this nonparticipant actually liked me, and that fact alone made it even worse.

As we wrapped up our meal he asked, "Can I tell you how I injured myself?"

Finally, he gave me something interesting to work with.

"Sure."

"Are you sure?"

"Sure I'm sure."

I wasn't sure.

"I was in a motorcycle accident last week. There was impact to my groin area, and, well . . . all the blood rushed to my Johnson. So I've had an erection since Friday. It won't go away. I've been to the hospital, and they are talking about surgery but it's risky. I don't want to attempt that for at least a month. I want to see if it will heal on its own." (Fair enough.)

He continued, "The good news about it is I would be a fun time in the sack right now. It would be like I was on Viagra—it won't go down, no matter what."

Are you fucking kidding me?

"So this is happening to you right now?" I asked.

"Yes."

Pause.

I finally settled on, "Thank you for such a generous offer, but I need to decline."

The check came to him. I politely asked, "May I help?"

"Yes. Thirty dollars, please."

A quick calculation and a stolen glance at the check revealed that amount was double the cost of what I'd had.

As my friend Alanis says, "You live, you learn."

A client, Simone, came to me for dating help. She'd had a traumatic experience and had been single and off the market for more than a decade. After working with me for one session, she decided to go on Match.com. She proudly announced in our second session, "I have my first date in over ten years, and it's tonight—a dinner date. He sounds amazing. He's forty-eight. He lives in Sausalito with a Golden Gate Bridge view, and he's a professional ethical hacker . . . and—"

"Wait, Simone, *no!*"

- If your date is centering the conversation on his junk, excuse yourself. Permanently. (Unless you want to have sex with him—in which case, listen and learn.)
- If you've injured yourself, have any ailments, rashes, breakouts, or swollen anything that could cast you in a severe negative light, take the week off from dating.
- If you're not hungry, don't order.
- If you're not into him, don't stay.

Part III

~~卌~~ ~~卌~~ ~~卌~~

After the First Date

Daunting decisions, fervent soul-searching, and

awkward encounters aside, one thing's for sure if you've reached this
point: You're doing it. You're dating!

But now what?

Where do you go from here?

What's next?

I wish I could tell you that starting is the hardest part. And
maybe it is—for some of us. For me, the hardest part came *after* I'd
finally gotten started. Dating is definitely as much about the journey
as it is about the destination, so let's look next at ways to make that
journey gentle (especially when we need to let others down), easy,
fun, and as successful as possible.

24

Not Interested in a Second Date?

Your first date is coming to a close. You've given him plenty of clues that although he's a nice person, you're just not interested in dating him, but you're so charming that his excitement has blinded him to your responses. As your date wraps up, he moves in for the good-night kiss. What do you do?

Do it anyway, to end the date?

No.

Quickly turn your head?

Noooo.

Fake sneezing while saying something about being contagious?

Also not a good idea.

Instead, be prepared. You can avoid the lean-in before it ever starts. As you're leaving the restaurant, take the lead in saying goodbye by walking a step or two in front of him. Near the car, turn and extend your hand so he can shake it, and as you do so, say, "It was very nice to meet you. Thank you for taking the time to come out and meet me." That should give those who are paying attention the (polite) hint that you're not interested in more.

If you're a hugger, you can do the same thing, only instead of extending the hand, you lean in for a side hug. As you pull back from the hug, be ready for a kiss in case it's on its way by moving your body out and away from him.

If you're new to dating, practice saying good-bye with a friend (including the hug or handshake) so that when you do it, you'll be confident in what will most likely be a slightly uncomfortable situation.

How to Say "No, Thank You"

Maybe it's right after the hug or maybe you realize it after another date or two—he's not the man for you but he's asking you out again.

How do you break it off? Do it quickly—Band-Aid style. Don't tell him yes when he asks, "Do you want to do this again?" and then dodge his phone calls. You're a big girl and he's a big boy. He can take rejection, and it's kinder for you to let him know up front. After all, would you like it if he said he'd call and never does?

Don't drag out the process. Don't keep dating him if you only plan to be his friend. It doesn't feel any better on their end than it does on ours.

Most of us aren't skilled at breaking it off because we don't want to hurt his feelings or be displeasing. This is natural. If you don't have a game plan on how to end a date like this, you might accidentally find yourself doing something you'd rather not in order to cut things off. The pressure can be intense, and your instinct will make you feel cornered. It's embarrassing, it's stressful—it sucks all-around.

If you find yourself in the position of playing the girl who's too nice to put her foot down, be kind to yourself. Your instincts drive you to be pleasing (or at least to avoid being displeasing) in almost every context. When we go against that grain, it's a victory, and when we don't, please realize you were simply following the orders your instincts were doling out. They're out to protect you. The orders they sometimes give are, "Do nothing. Say nothing. You need to get out of this situation safely." Freezing or saying nothing but complying (while not wonderful for you) is nothing to beat yourself up for later. You did the best you could, friend. And you are not alone.

Again, I think the best thing you can do to prevent this is to practice with a friend. Here are some lines that work effectively, and while it might sting in the moment, it won't make him feel worse about himself because they aren't personal. Pick one or two and take them for a spin with a friend playing the role of your date:

"We're not (quite) a match."
"I had a lovely time, but I don't see a fit here."
"I don't see a matching future for the two of us."
"I don't feel enough of a connection."
The above are all phrases men can relate to. If he persists, try:
"I'm looking for something different."
If he persists still:
"That's all I have to say."

It's more than likely you won't have to get that far. Once they've heard "we're not a match," most men don't care to know why. That's generally a woman thing. We want to know why because we think that if they tell us why, then we can change ourselves to become what he prefers or that then we'll know what to "fix" about ourselves so that we can avoid future rejections. Don't go there.

If he does end up being one of the dudes who's looking for the "what's wrong with me?" type of answer, repeat, kindly but firmly, "That's all I have to say." And if you'd like, you could add, "And my answer won't serve you." You're basically saying, "I'm sorry you're disappointed, and I understand that. But this won't work for me or for you." Not bad, not wrong, nothing to fix. It's not personal. Does a Toyota have the right to be mad when you pick a Honda instead? No. You're just looking for something different.

The men I've talked to about this said they don't care if you think he's a great guy. Telling him all the things you like about him will not help or make the pill easier to swallow. Don't puff him up with what's great about him when you don't want to be his girlfriend. And let's face it: when you're online dating, you aren't looking for new friends. So be quick, rip off the Band-Aid, and be as kind as possible because as you know, this part isn't fun for anyone.

Seattle Nate said, "Hearing I'm great and understanding why I'm not her man do nothing for me. I'd rather just know up front that it's not going to work for her and be able to move on."

The next two dates are examples of when to leave dates at the right time—one when I left a date before it even started and the other where I should have left and didn't.

Date #2
Tom Waits Will Have to Wait

Setting: Drinks and dinner at McNear's Saloon
& Dining House, Petaluma, CA

What's a single, urban girl living in wine country to do for dates? If men who drive a pickup or sport a yoga mat for their briefcase aren't your scene (not that there's anything wrong with that), there's only one place to go: online.

Date #2 was at the start of my online experiment. I'd recently joined Match.com to find my man, and I decided to date outside my comfort zone but not outside my geographic location. Age and location—those were my criteria because in all my years, I'd realized one thing: left to my own devices, I could not trust my judgment in picking men. I did a fine job with a husband of twelve years, but outside of that, I was unskilled.

Date #2 told me he was fifty, owned several hundred cattle acres in the county, and ran a local dairy farm. Sonoma is a large county, with hundreds of thousands of residents, but I got to thinking, do you know who lives out in this county besides Date #2? Tom Waits, one of the most influential experimental rock musicians of the last thirty-odd years. His distinctive, raspy, bourbon-soaked voice spins wild tale after wild tale surrounded in a creative mix of jazz, anger, and bizarre, haunting circus music. *Rain Dogs* is my favorite album. Anyway, Tom is a genius, and he's one of the residents living out in the countryside somewhere in the wine country. Maybe Tom shared the fence with Date #2. If so, I not only wanted to date this man but I also wanted to marry him. That's right—so I could be Mrs. Tom-Waits's-Next-Door-Neighbor. That's what I'd expect you to call me. My new country life was going to be so outlandishly fantastic, I might even learn how to milk a cow and everything.

"Let's not write back and forth; let's meet for dinner," he wrote.

"Okay. Tell you what. Since you don't know Sonoma that well, I will come to your town so you can pick one of your favorite places." I hoped he'd pick a place Tom Waits goes to on weekends. I know, I know, I'm shameless.

He said yes. Mission accomplished. I was officially an online dater.

I arrived at McNear's after Date #2 did, and as we waited for our table, we ordered drinks at the bar. Double Scotch for him. Within seconds, he downed it. I'd had one sip of my pinot. I frantically tried to recall his online profile. Did he mark the box "social drinker" or was it "drinks regularly/heavily"? Maybe not a red flag, but I'm putting a pink Post-it note on that one.

We'd hardly made any small talk at all when he informed me he'd like me to move into his home on the range. He described the décor: a gaudy oversized ranch with various dead animal heads lining the walls. I'd be working for him from home, apparently—kind of a girlfriend–personal assistant–milkmaid situation—so owning my own travel agency (as I did before I sold it several years after this date) will have to go by the wayside. I'd known him less than ten minutes.

Our smiling hostess arrived with two menus tucked under her right arm and a cordless phone in her left hand, eager to seat us at our table. I didn't move. She narrowed her eyes and her expression turned to one of irritated impatience. Clearly she had better things to do. This was the moment—in or out. Be brave, Wendy, be brave. The tips of my fingers slid along the piping of his cowboy shirt at his shoulder to softy get his attention while I said, "Thank you so much for the drink. We won't be having dinner. We're not a match." And I was G-O-N-E.

My heart felt like it was going to race me to my car as I sprinted away from the restaurant. I dove in and started the ignition, and as I pulled away, the racing feeling began to dissipate and was replaced by a slow, steady sense of relief.

My cozy next-door friendship with Tom Waits will just have to wait.

What I did right: I not only left but I left at the right time. I knew we weren't a fit and found that perfect time to skate out before food was ordered and we were committed to pay for something other than a drink. (I had already covered my bar tab.)

What I did wrong: I went to his town. He could have come to mine. We could have met halfway. I planned dinner instead of drinks when I didn't know whether we had ninety minutes of interesting conversation between us. I blame Tom Waits for that oversight.

Date #12
Too Good to Be True? (Yep.)

Setting: Drinks at XYZ Bar at the W Hotel,
San Francisco, CA

He seemed too good to be true. Six-foot-one, average body, CEO of a prestigious Manhattan company splitting his time between the New York, London, and San Francisco offices. Living a glamorous multi-city life? Yes, please. (I thrived on the fantasy of what our life looks like together, remember?)

We'd talked a bit by phone and he was pushy, but aren't all New Yorkers? I didn't let this dampen my daydreams. I had to land this one. I bought a new summer dress, got a full manicure/pedicure, and even had my hair washed and blown out professionally so I would look my absolute "right out of the salon" best.

The plan: meet at XYZ in the W Hotel for a glass of champagne and then move on to dinner.

Right outside the front door of XYZ, a man stepped out of a cab and quickly moved toward me, hollering in his New York accent, "Wendy. Great timing; I'm here." Was he talking to me? It couldn't be. He looked nothing like his photo, and his stats were all wrong. Instead of six-foot-one with an average body, I was looking down at five-foot-one and a weight somewhere around three hundred pounds. CEO? He sported wrinkled tan Dockers-style pleated pants, a faded purple shirt, and a black jacket with a button missing on the right sleeve. His mismatched suit looked more Salvation Army than Armani.

Here's where I made my first real mistake. We walked inside together. Every second I stayed on this date after this moment was a mistake. This man had lied to me before we'd ever met. Presenting oneself inaccurately is not wishful thinking; it's lying, plain and simple.

Now, normally I would have found a way to slip out of it sooner than this, like on the sidewalk right in front of XYZ. A polite "I'm sorry. We're not quite a match. Let's not waste each other's time," would have been the right thing to say. However, once we were inside and champagne arrived, he told me the story of how his car had broken down and he didn't want to miss our date so he took a taxi in from Palo Alto. That's close to two hundred dollars round-trip. If he went through that kind of expense, I owed it to him, right? (Wrong.)

We sat through idle conversation until it was time to find a restaurant. On the Embarcadero, we found a lovely spot with a view of the Bay Bridge. He ordered an appetizer and two entrees then asked what I was having. About two-thirds through our lengthy meal at this four-star restaurant, he started flatulating and kept it up for the rest of the evening. These weren't quiet little pops only I could hear. His indiscretions rattled the industrial steel-framed picture windows and raised a cloud of stink so pungent it could have killed a cat (or me from embarrassment alone). All this was put forth without regard for the other diners, acknowledgment, or apology. Now, I understand this could have been a one-off—unusual gas from something he ate or even a chronic issue. Either way, while that's terrible for him, it was torture for me and every other diner in the hall.

As he walked me back to my car, he started to look for a cab. "Boy, was it expensive to get here. In fact, the whole evening was . . ." Before he could say another word, I heard myself say in somewhat of a resigned tone, "I can give you a ride back to Palo Alto." *Crap. Now I'm going to be trapped in my car with Fart Man.*

Reluctantly, I drove him back to his home. Once there, I needed to use the facilities, so I asked to make a trip inside. The place was filthy, and from the front door to the bathroom, there were tall, stacked pathways of junk. He was a hoarder.

Getting out of that house was tricky. If you have ever done something that you didn't want to do just to end the date without confrontation, know this: you're not alone. I was trapped in that house much longer than I wanted to be.

What I did wrong: I stayed on the date. This date should have been over within the first ninety seconds. Yes, it would have been uncomfortable for me to end it, especially knowing how far he had traveled. It would have been difficult to put my hand lightly on his shoulder and say in my softest voice, "I'm sorry. I know you've traveled a long way, but we're not a match." But it certainly wouldn't have been as uncomfortable as it was by night's end.

If a date grossly misrepresents themselves (lies) to you in their profile, you owe them nothing. Sure, you could end it immediately with a nice "we're not a fit" but my BFF Leslie says, "There's a big difference between nice and kind." It would be a kindness to tell them the truth. Try "Hey, you're not who you say you are from your online profile. I'm not staying for this date."

25

Stalking Your New Date Is Never a Smart Idea

So you met him online. He's amazing. He has qualities you admire and he's totally sexy too. Good for you. Here comes the hardest part: after the first date, you're going to want to visit him online. You're curious, and your brain wants to gather as much information about him as possible. You think maybe if you reread that profile again, you'll learn something new. Plus, when you visit his profile, you feel connected, and that makes you all warm and fuzzy, right?

You like him. You think he's terrific. You feel happy. So you do a drive-by online and notice his status says "online now." Instantly you experience a moment of terror. Yes, it's true. He's looking at other women. Other women who could out-attract you. You just know it. He's talking to the woman who has every quality he wants that you don't. They could be emailing back and forth right now. You can forget any plans you had with him for the upcoming weekend because he's moving on. Oh wait, he hasn't set a future date with you yet? The little insecurity elves dancing a jig inside your chest just stepped up the pace times ten.

Somehow you muddle along. The two of you keep dating, and when you feel like connecting with him, you check his status. It seems like he's always online and he's not emailing you at the rate you'd like. After experiencing this repeatedly, one day you log on for a visit, see the "ONLINE NOW" status, and you blurt out, "Fuck you!"

It's official. This process has turned you into one of *those* online daters—one who's irritated with him when he hasn't done one thing wrong.

Raise your hand if you know what I'm talking about.

The last time I encountered this problem I was two months into seeing a man I was wild about. Unbeknownst to anyone else, I'd become a lunatic, mostly because I wasn't getting the attention I needed from him. I ended the craziness by going off the site completely. I didn't tell him I was leaving it, and I didn't ask him to, either. I just quietly took down my profile.

One thing that makes us feel safe, loved, and sane as human beings is connection with the people we care about. Stated simply, when you connect with your (potential) mate, you instinctively feel safe. When you go online and you see he's not connecting with you and instead he's connecting with other women, you lose that feeling of safety and warmth. Hopping online for a drive-by is not kind to your spirit and you lose your capacity to be your best self.

You might think that looking at him online isn't that big a deal. And to be honest, it's not a big deal . . . when you're looking at the ones you don't like that much. I recommend you try hard—very, very hard—to avoid peeking. The truth is, it's not going to help your situation. In fact, it could be outright damaging it. It's one of the things that drive women off a site, away from online dating, and away from potentially compatible partners.

Most daters use dating site apps on their smartphone. Once logged in for a quick check, the phone will keep him logged in for the better half of the day, making it appear as if he's always online. Keep in mind that you're dating a single person. And single people are free to date anyone they wish (just like you!), as often as they wish. When you're dating someone off-line, he could be dating other women and you don't have access to witness it. I believe wholeheartedly that, in this case, ignorance is bliss.

Need another reason not to be a stalker? On most sites, your voyeurism is public. That's right, creeper, he can see you looking at him! Some sites are smart enough to charge you for a privacy feature, so you have to pay to stalk privately. Do you really want to make a dating site rich because you can't control your impulses? (Says the woman who paid $9.99 a month for the privacy option on OkCupid. Hey, I write what I know.)

My friend Leslie had a brilliant perspective on this topic. When I described this phenomenon to her, she said, "Oh, so you're snooping. You mean you just poke your nose into his private business?"

Holy shit! I'd never thought of it this way. So in real life, I'm not a snooper. In my forty-some-odd years on this planet, I've never read a man's email, checked his phone, or looked up anything on him. Normally, I'm not compelled to do this, and frankly, I don't understand women who do. Even if I felt I had something to concern myself with, I wouldn't go about getting the information behind his back. I'd sort it with him directly or sort myself out. So it was shocking to see that even I (a non-snooper in real life) have in fact stuck my nose right where it didn't belong online. It's none of our business. And let's face it, snooping rarely turns out well.

I have to give mad props to my girl Leslie for her brilliant insight. I never did it again. Not that it was any less tempting, mind you, but once I saw his profile as his personal business, it was an integrity issue; I just couldn't do it.

So what does a smart dater do instead? Start by printing or downloading his profile. That way you have access to all that juicy information you crave anytime. You can drag the photos right off the website and onto your computer. And voilà—you have your very own file on your hard drive for handy reference.

Or you can hide (not block) him from view by deleting him out of your search results once you've printed his profile. After the drop and drag, go get yourself a bigger life. Use that time you'd spend stalking him to go to a café and read a book, take a hike, see a film, or have a drink with girlfriends. Here's a novel idea: use the time to keep dating other men. You're single, remember?

So here's what we learned:

- Being a stalker is uncool, and snooping into his personal business starts with "visiting."
- Your time is precious and valuable.
- Viewing his profile over and over will burn you out and make you hate the dating process ever so slightly more than you already do.

26

Decoding "You Deserve to Be with Someone Who Can Make You Happy"

Men who want to date you will want to provide for you. Just go with me on this one. I'm not saying he's paying next month's rent or running out to buy you that electric fondue maker you've been eyeing, but he will want to contribute to your life if you end up being his girl. He'll be looking to see if he can afford you. He won't ask what you need, instead he'll listen for clues based on the four areas below and from these he will eventually sort you potentially in or out.

1. He will account for what he believes all women need.
2. He figures you need what you already have.
3. He assesses the lifestyle you've had in the past. (For instance, he'll consider even your previous marriage or what you had in childhood.)
4. He determines what you need based on what you talk about.

If you're dating someone and you're both nuts about each other but he determines he can't provide for you, he will most likely end it without even thinking to talk to you about it. He might end it by saying something like, "I don't think I can make you happy." Done.

Would you like to know how to avoid this?

Be up front about what you can provide for yourself and what you hope your mate to provide. Now, I don't mean whip out a list of what you need on the first date, but if you're going to talk about the house you bought last year and the brand-new BMW you bought yesterday when you know he drives a beat-up pickup truck (that you think he looks sexy in), this can be a problem for both of you.

Am I telling you to downplay your lifestyle? Nope! Most men have no problem with women being more successful monetarily. My experience and research have shown me that it's a smidge generational overall, with the young pumpkins being cooler about it than the silver haired foxes. But whoever you're dating, let him know the situation. Tell the truth. Collaborate. This is the twenty-first century, after all.

Here's an example script for talking about money with a new man:

You: "Yeah, I love my house. When I got my inheritance, I put the whole thing into it, so now I only owe about two hundred thousand and the mortgage payment is fifteen hundred bucks a month. Awesome, right?"

Or:

"I enjoy my job, and I love being good at what I do. I feel lucky. I'm not looking for a partner to match my income. What I do need is a partner who can be there to comfort me when I've had a bad day. And I'm looking for someone to have a lot of fun with. If you work all the time, that wouldn't bode well for our free time. Having good times with you is way more important to me than spending more time on bringing in more money."

In the olden days, it was simpler for everyone. We got married so he could put a roof over our heads and we could bring up the kids and make delicious pie. But while that's still a valid deal for some of us, that's no longer what others of us are looking for.

Our culture changed but nobody issued us a memo on how to deal with the update of partnership model options. So it's up to you to be accountable for sharing with him what you expect and what you don't require so he doesn't guess inaccurately and run away saying, "I won't be able to make you happy. You deserve to be with someone who can make you happy." Happiness in modern relationships is all about what both people can do to help each other be happy, and understanding where the other is coming from on this topic is essential to success.

27

Hey, Smart, Successful Girl, You Don't Intimidate Him

One of our favorite phrases as a single woman is, "Men find me intimidating, I think it's because I'm successful at work." Or, "My PhD is too intimidating to the men I date. I don't think they can handle it." Smarty-Pants Girl, I have some bad news for you: you are not intimating to men. I've done the social research to back it up and I couldn't find a single man who felt intimidated by you. Straight from the horse's mouth, here's what men had to say (over and over and over again) on this topic:

Q: "Why are men so intimidated by a strong, smart, and successful woman?"

A: "They aren't, unless they're fourteen years old."

When a woman tells me, "He was intimidated by me because I'm smart and successful," or "Do I have to dumb it down?" I want to lovingly tell her the truth: "No, he's not intimidated. He's just not interested in you." I usually hold my tongue, but I won't hold it here. He's not intimidated; he's either getting attitude from you or you're treating your interactions as a competition rather than a collaboration.

Or maybe you're not being open to him contributing to your life, 'cuz, you know, you got this.

Men aren't intimidated by success, smarts, and strength; those characteristics are not inherently intimidating. What men are put off by is an attitude of complete self-sufficiency. There's a big difference between "I've got my life together. Go, me!" and "I've got everything together, so what do I need you for?" Our society has trained many of us to mistake self-reliance for self-confidence. No one's 100 percent self-reliant, and that's okay. Think of it this way: if you're independent and there's no room for anyone else to provide anything in your life (because you've got it all covered), then there's no space for him. I'm not saying you should be a hot mess. Men love strong, capable women—and we love being strong and capable. In fact, wouldn't it make sense to partner with someone strong, smart, and competent so you can take on the world together and have the biggest, bestest life ever? Um, can I get a hell yes? Getting to that biggest, bestest life involves—you guessed it—a lot of communication and cooperation so that both parties feel they're getting their needs met—and that includes your man's need to provide for you in some way. Most guys want a woman who will let him in and be excited about the many gifts he has to give in whatever form those gifts come.

If your lifestyle doesn't sync up with that traditional 1950s model where your guy's the breadwinner and you're the housewife, especially if you make piles of money—like oodles more than he does—you might want to consider setting any perceived or real tension between you two about this at ease by using this simple phrase:

"I'm so thankful that you provide _____."

My guess is Oprah had to have this conversation (or something similar) with her partner, Stedman Graham. Us strong, powerful, successful women can do a lot of things for ourselves, but do you know what you can't do? You can't listen to yourself give yourself a different perspective. You can't lovingly witness your own life. You can't support and congratulate yourself in a meaningful way when you work hard. And for sure, you won't tell yourself it's time to take a break. How easy is it for you to have your own back, or inspire yourself to be a better person? These things are delicious when they're provided by someone who loves you. It makes them shine all the more brighter.

28

When It's Time to Take a Break

While dating—especially dating online—there will be periods where you want to quit. You'll be dating when you're not clear-headed, when the whole thing seems depressing, intolerable, and not worth it. When this happens, it's time for a time-out reboot so you can remember to look at the endgame: living with your partner, feeling fully appreciated, and having the love and connection you desire.

If you date for any length of time, you'll be susceptible to burnout. It's a fact. This is when you want to use your dating allies because they can help you recognize the signs that it's time to take a break before things get out of hand. Pull them into this conversation early so that you're not dealing with burnout alone.

Here are a few warning signs that it's break time:

- When you start to think that every single person out there is a liar who doesn't represent themselves as they really are.
- When you're experiencing numerous wrong turns, one after another—anything from experiencing everyday dick moves to being the victim of a fake-emergency flee.

👄 After experiencing humiliating rejection, particularly miserable dates, several dates in a row with no connection, or wildly mismatched pairings, or when you encounter those who only want to fuck you—I don't need to tell you that this can be a drag.

I hear you, sister, and again, you're not alone. One time when I quit, I wrote on my dating blog, "I quit. For reals. I'm exhausted. In the last year, I've viewed 7,183 men's profiles. I've been viewed by 4,264 men on Match.com. I just cancelled my subscription. Forever? Who knows . . . for now, definitely."

This entry came after First Date #88. Little did I know I still had 33 dates to go!

During my dating process, people often asked, "You did all that dating but you didn't find him. Would you still recommend Match.com? Online dating in general?" Here's the thing: with all those dates, I did meet someone—108 someones (out of my 121 first dates, I met 108 of them online). And I eventually did meet "my" someone, also online. So yes, I highly recommend sticking with online dating, even though the process can be exhausting at times.

And still, sometimes a break is in order. There are times it's best to put your account on hold, climb into bed, pull the covers over your head, and watch *Law & Order* reruns. Just remember that while giving yourself a hard-earned and much-needed break from dating can be healthy—necessary, even—getting back up and into the game is equally important. My advice on breaks boils down to this: Take one when you feel you need one. Care for yourself in whatever ways your mind, body, and soul need and have a reliable support system in place to help get you back in the groove when break time's over. Never underestimate the value of your dating allies!

29

Why Didn't He Call?

Here it is: the big one. A dating phenomenon that makes good women everywhere feel like giving up on dating forever.

I don't know any woman who's dated and never asked herself, "Why didn't he call?" I can't count how many times I've asked this question and how many times my inner critic's offered up a cruel laundry list of possibilities, most of which, upon reflection, ranged from ridiculous to downright insane.

When it comes to dating, here is what's in our power to do:

- Obtain a date
- Show up for the date
- Present yourself as yourself (you know, who you really are, not who you think he wants you to be)

If you do these things and he didn't call you after that, girl, you did your very best. He didn't call because he's not your man. It's easy for me to say, I know. And I'm not disregarding your hurt feelings and dashed hopes. I've suffered the heartbreak of waiting and waiting and waiting for that call too. From time to time it happens, and when it does, I'm sorry.

I'm sorry you got your hopes up.

I'm sorry his not calling has hurt your feelings.

I'm sorry you were nearly certain your partner had finally arrived.

I'm sorry he seemed like he was a perfect match for you.

I'm sorry he didn't see it too.

If you could find out exactly why he didn't call, I promise you that it wouldn't be any consolation. Men have lots of reasons for not calling, much like we have lots of reasons for not wanting a second date. Some of his reasons may be:

- He likes you and you had a memorable date, but you weren't quite who he was looking for.
- He could tell you were looking for one thing, and he wasn't interested in providing that at this stage of his life. (In other words, he didn't feel that you two had matching futures.)
- There was something he heard from you that was a deal-breaker for him.
- He is fresh out of a relationship and thought he was ready to date but now realizes he's not there yet. (In other words, it's a case of bad timing.)
- He is enchanted by you but knows he isn't ready for the real deal that you are.

Whatever his reason was, the point remains the same: he didn't call, and while this can be a big disappointment, it's not going to derail you from your goal. The only thing that will cure this particular ache is time (and a new man wouldn't hurt, either). Consider this: he didn't call you because he is not your man. Do you know how you can tell if a man is your man? You can tell because your man calls.

But why don't they call to break it off? It would be the courteous thing to do, after all. Get this: most men don't call because they want to spare your feelings. (Really.)

"What?" you yelp. "Spare my feelings? Doesn't he know I'm waiting for his call and I'm feeling worse with every second that passes?"

No. He doesn't know that. Men think that you're continuing on with your life as it was before your date with him. Most men don't understand our amazing ability to multitask, which includes keeping part of our attention on him nearly 24/7, even when we're busy. He knows that the two of you aren't right for each other and he doesn't want to bring you bad news in the middle of your perfectly nice day. He sincerely doesn't want to cause you any hurt feelings, so in his mind, if he doesn't call, he's doing it to spare you the interruption and inconvenience of being upset. (Truly.)

Another reason a man may not call is because he doesn't feel he owes it to you. After only a date or two, he is not in a relationship with you. He thinks it's highly inefficient and, frankly, kind of weird to contact someone to tell her he's not going to contact her anymore. Again, this one stings—especially if you're into him—but it doesn't reflect on anything but the fact that he's not the one for you.

You know what? When he doesn't call, you should pout. Pout it out for a couple of days. And after that, consider that he did you a favor. By not calling, he is helping you sort faster. That may not seem like a blessing in the moment, but is it ever.

A Player Move

Then there's the "let me give you my number" player phenomenon. This one is mostly generational. It tends to happen with men right up to around forty. Your number? Forget it. An ego stroke is what he's after. He'll want to see if you want to play with him. If you call him, chances are you will never receive a return call because he wasn't that interested in the first place.

If you've got a confident (and slightly cocky) young man standing in front of you for the first time and if he's interested, then he should ask for your number. If you have to offer yours or he offers his but doesn't ask for yours in return, don't get your hopes up. If you like him and want to play it out, here's what to do:

- He offers his number.
- Instead of writing it down, put it right into your phone.
- Hit "call" while you're with him.
- When his phone rings, say: "There. Now you have mine if you want to give me a call."

Some men will offer you their number or email address because they do like you but they aren't sure whether you're equally interested. You're going to have to navigate the number exchange by paying attention to what hints he's dropping about his true personality and goals.

Back to the whole "But does he *like* like me?" question. When you're looking for a mate, keeping an eye on that simple question is incredibly important. And how much does he like you? Men who like you will pursue you. You'll see the signs, and if you don't, it's time to let him go. Let's start paying attention to this from the beginning.

Ten Things to Do to Take Care of You

So he doesn't call. Knowing he's not your man is informative, but it sucks! How do you manage through it? Here are my top ten ways.

Sulk

I mean really sulk. Be sad. Eat ice cream in front of the latest crappy romantic comedy you couldn't be bothered to see during its first run at the theater. Be angry. Cry. Don't try to bypass the process or rise above it; it will bite you in the ass later. Create an end time for the wallowing and stick to it, enlisting the help of your dating allies as needed. I'd try not to let it go on for longer than ten days (and I don't mean ten business days).

Tell Someone Who Will Understand

Don't suffer alone. Tell the person who will be most understanding and can love you up the 'most. Use your dating allies for this. Set them up to listen to you by saying something like, "Friend, I need your help. I want to tell you something. All I need from you to help me is to listen. And maybe from time to time, say, 'That's terrible,' or 'I'm sorry,' or 'I love you,' or, 'He's an asshat.'"

> Please agree with me.
> Please don't try to solve this problem.
> Please don't give me advice.
> Please don't tell me that my guy will come along when I least
>   expect it or anything along those lines.
> All I need you to do is listen, commiserate, and love me.

Once you've shared your guidelines with your dating ally, let it rip. Don't leave anything unsaid. A word to the wise: married or coupled women are often not suitable at this unless they've spent a lot of time being single earlier in their life. We women tend to have amnesia about this stuff once we're in a relationship, and we give unhelpful advice like, "You should be happy and enjoy being single while you still are!" Nope, that's not what we need to hear, no matter how well meant the sentiment may be.

Visualize

Visualize your best life ever, your favorite version of your future. Go full-blown fantasy. Spend a whole afternoon daydreaming. And be sure that this future doesn't include him in it.

Get Physical

Hit the dance or yoga studio, gym, or hiking trail. Physical activity will help you work him out of your body and mind. (It will also help you work off all that ice cream.)

Take Salt Baths

Take a long, hot bath in Epsom salt. You may have to do this daily until you're feeling better. Your local drugstore probably carries Epsom salts. I like the lavender kind (it's yummy). Imagine that the salt is literally pulling your sadness out of your body (because that's exactly what's happening).

Get Touched by a Man

A professional massage by a male massage therapist, if you feel comfortable doing so, works miracles.

Nurture Yourself with Flowers

Buy yourself a dozen red roses. Your local grocery store most likely has them for between ten and twenty bucks.

Let Your Men Love You

Let the men in your life who love you contribute to you. This could be your brother, your father, a friend, or an ex turned loving friend. Ask him to tell you what he thinks is amazing about you.

Think Happy Thoughts

Tell yourself:

"He's not my match. My match is coming."
"He did me a favor by not calling."
"I'm making space for my partner to come."
"I'm closer than I was before I knew him."

Use a Heart Healing Technique

Once you've been hurt, disappointed, disrespected, or dishonored, it's very easy to close up and become hardened by the experience. You may find it nearly impossible to stay open and vulnerable until you can take the time to heal and restore yourself. You need to clear out the harm from your body and spirit. If you don't clear away the hurt and disappointment, you might want to give up dating forever. Or you'll keep going but you won't be able to be generous or vulnerable or find any joy in the process. One man I knew called women like this "crispy," as in we've been burned one too many times. I've had my share of leaving my love life in the oven too long, and I bet you have too.

This happens to all of us, and one thing you can do to clear it out is Heart Healing.

Before I teach you how to do this, I want you to know my story. I first learned of the Heart Healing practice through PAX Programs. As a staff person it's important that I road-test the material and exercises, and I continually do independent research to really own what I learn as new discoveries come to light.

Heart Healing came along as an exercise to heal oneself from almost any injury to the heart. At first the process seemed stupid to me—way too simple and easy to actually work. I mean, come on; I say something, someone says they're sorry (and not even the person who caused me the pain in the first place), and my pain goes away? Get real! I halfheartedly tried it, but it wasn't my thing. I let it go. I didn't have to do or teach this stupid exercise. Until . . . well, until I was d-e-s-p-e-r-a-t-e.

I decided to try it as a last-ditch effort because I felt like I was walking around with the weight of 120 men on my back. Before this moment I thought I could take care of myself, dust myself off, and start fresh. I thought I was a self-cleaning oven. Not true. When I finally hollered "uncle," I called on my friend Vince because having a man say he was sorry for the atrocities of other men might be a big bang for my buck. I was right. We blocked sixty minutes but ended up spending a concentrated ninety minutes on the telephone going through offense after offense and we cleared out dozens and dozens and dozens of past date injuries. Toward the end, we were doing them in batches, "For all the men who . . ." The next day I felt so much lighter, and within days of our session, I met my partner, Dave, Date #121.

When you're ready to clear it out and be healed, ask someone you trust to do the following exercise with you over the phone or in person (not in text or email).

The Basics of the Heart Healing Technique

Set your healer up to do this Heart Healing exercise with you by laying out the instructions before you start. Let your healer know their job is to

- Ask if you're ready to be healed.
- Ask who the person is (first name and relationship).
- Ask you if you're ready to begin.
- When you start, they repeat exactly what you said, starting with "I'm sorry" or "I'm so sorry."
- They need to give you space to breathe and to see if you need anything else. Have them ask, "Is there anything more?" If yes, repeat the process again until there's nothing left.

Your part is to

- Answer yes when you're ready to be healed.
- Tell them who the person is (first name and relationship).
- Answer when you're ready to begin.

- When you start, tell them what the offense is—what this person did to hurt your feelings, dishonor you, disrespect you, or upset you. The description of the offense can be brief. You need to get to the point without telling the whole story.
- They will ask, "Is there anything more?" And if there is, go ahead and say more or add detail if you feel it will help.

You may need to hear it in another way. For example, you may say, "He hurt my feelings when he said I wasn't as smart as other women he'd dated." And when that doesn't work, if you're not feeling better after the healing part of that takes place, you can go back and rephrase: "He disrespected me when he compared me to other women; he made me feel inferior." Let them heal you with the rephrased version. If you're still not feeling healed, look to see how else that same offense could be expressed. Repeat as many times as you feel necessary.

Special notes: none of the offenses need to be justified in any way. The offender may not even know you were hurt. That's not the point. The point is that if you're affected by something that happened, then you need to clear it out of your heart; therefore, what you're saying is valid. Also, your healer has no special power but rather is simply providing his or her empathy and love for you. It's up to you and your will to heal your pain. In other words, your healer can only heal you if you allow it.

Here's a sample conversation so you can get an idea of how this might look:

Healer: "Are you ready to start? Are you willing to be healed?"

You: "Yes."

Healer: "Okay, I'm ready for you. I'm ready to listen."

Both of you take a breath and pay attention to each other. Treat this like what you're doing can make a significant difference in your life, because it can if you're willing.

You: "Okay, the person is my last date, Jim. Jim hurt my feelings when he said he'd call me the next day and he never called."

Healer: "I'm so sorry Jim hurt your feelings when he said he'd call the next day and he never called. (Breathe.) I'm so sorry about that."

Take it in. Breathe.

Healer continues: "Is there anything else about that?"

You: "Yes. He said he really liked me, and now I feel like he was putting me on. Maybe he was just getting through the date. I feel so stupid."

Notice the lack of detail. It's about how you feel, not all the details of what he said and what you said and what happened.

Healer: "I am so sorry he said he really liked you and he didn't follow through. He didn't call. I'm so sorry. And I'm sorry he made you feel like he might have been putting you on to get through the date. I'm sorry you feel that way. I'm so sorry he made you feel stupid."

Note that to do this exercise, it's okay to say, "Jim made me feel . . ." even though we are responsible for our own interpretations and feelings. While your head might know something intellectually, your heart feels like he made it happen, so it's fine for you and your healer to say it like that. You do not need to be accountable for anything for this process. You're healing your heart.

The healer continues: "Is there anything else about that?"

If there is, continue with every offense until you feel like you have cleared them all out. It's also fine if it leads to something else. Maybe this happened three dates back with another guy. Or when you felt abandoned by your father. You could think of it as a ball of thread and you're pulling one string at a time with each repeated incident.

This is something you can teach your dating ally so you can provide it for each other. It's also something to teach an open-minded and willing male friend so he can apologize on behalf of other men.

Please don't ask the offender of your hurt feelings to be the healer. Think of it this way: if a car hit you, you wouldn't ask the driver of that car to set your leg in a cast; you'd see a doctor. If you don't have a person in your life to provide Heart Healing, you can set a coaching appointment through wendyspeaks.com for a private one-on-one session. My coaches are trained specifically in Heart Healing.

Heart Healing is one powerful tool that frees you from your past and gives you a shot at being restored to your former shininess. It doesn't just mask the pain. Through this process you can completely erase it. (I disappeared a two-year hurt—Date #60: Bubble Boy—in two minutes flat.) After you've healed yourself, when you meet your match, he has a fresh, clean, kind, and supple you—the best version of you.

Your Inner Critic Is Not Your Friend

You have a voice in your head. I have one too. I call it my inner critic. We've been talking about this voice a lot, and we're about to talk about it some more.

My inner critic lives on the upper-left-side of my head, just behind my ear. That's where I hear her talk to me. Her voice sounds exactly like mine, and she's never nice. She pretends she's looking out for me, like she wants me to be my best self and the way she's going to get me there is by criticizing everything I do—you know, so I can be a better person. She lets me know where I'm failing: as a partner, a daughter, a friend, a dog mom, an entrepreneur—in nearly every area of my life. Can you relate? Her standard is perfection, but I told her a long time ago that I was far from perfect so we weren't going to play that game. But she still tries.

Do you know where she gets us the most? On the dating field. Don't listen to her. She's not your helpful friend. She means well, but she's misguided because her standard is perfection, and perfection is not obtainable; and let's face it: it's boring.

She'll tell you why you're never going to get your guy by telling you what's wrong with you. She'll tell you why you should give up on dating: "You're too fat. Jump off the dating sites until you've dropped that weight." Or, "You're too old. They're only looking for women at most ten years younger than you are."

She'll tell you why he didn't call back, and her answer is never an empowering one.

She'll recap every date you've been on. She conducts sportscaster commentaries of your dates complete with slo-mo replays and big sloppy marker circles and arrows on the screen behind your eyes. She'll tell you every single perceived misstep you made. She'll tell you what you should have done instead, what you shouldn't have worn, and she'll say things like, "Oh no, why did you tell *that* story?" Or, "You laughed too loud." Or, "Did he see you in bright light in *those* pants? OMG." Her list of how you blew it is unending.

Again: Don't listen to her, girl. Listen to me. If you showed up and you were yourself, then even if you laughed too loud or talked too much or you can't believe you told *that* story, it's all fine. If he's your man, he'll come back. If he's not, he won't, and it's all good because your man (who's coming) loves you just as you are: donkey laugh, extra fat roll in that one spot, inappropriate storytelling, and all. You're holding out for the man who loves all of you. Don't let that crazy lady in your head pick you apart. She may sound like you, but she's not you. Remember that.

32

Keeping Pace

So far, this book has mostly been about ways to help you have what you need: tools for narrowing down your dating pool, navigating the online and in-person dating landscape, being a courteous citizen on a date, and taking care of yourself when things don't go the way you want or need them to go.

Have you noticed that there's been very little of the dirty S-word, strategy? I'm anti-strategy. Remember the book from the 1990s called *The Rules*? I'm not a fan of rules for many reasons, but mostly because following rules to be strategic or manipulative so you can "catch" him and keep him takes you further away from your authentic self, and when you're single and dating, it's hard enough to try to maintain your authenticity. The desire to find your partner is constantly coaxing you into being someone you think he might like better, and when the pressure's on, being yourself is the last thing that comes to mind. If you want to find him and keep him, one thing that most men love is authenticity. I guess I'm secretly strategizing for you to find your man by being your authentic self.

So this, lovely sister of mine, is the first and only taste of strategy you'll get out of me.

When you're Dating with a capital *D* (you're at least a couple of dates in and things are going well) and you're mad about him, it's important to pay attention to his continued level of participation. If you'd like, you can try responding at the same pace he's contacting you. I'm not saying match him move for move. What I am saying is if he wants to reach out to you once a week and you want to reach out to him once an hour, you may have a compatibility problem.

It's important to pay just the slightest bit of attention to his pacing for the following three reasons:

1. If you're calling, texting, and emailing him every five minutes, you aren't allowing any space for the creation of tension. Now, I know most of us hate tension. Tension is uncomfortable and makes us wonder if the relationship is slipping from our fingers. But tension can be positive. For one, the distance and silence can cause sexual tension, and that's usually a fire you want to feed.

2. Another reason to let him do most of the leading is that you'll see how much he generates all on his own. This is the start of seeing exactly how interested he is in you. You want to see if he takes the lead and plans dates, calls you to talk you to sleep, sends you flirty texts, and makes you mix tapes. It's important to show him your interest as well, of course, but there's a lot to say for letting him take your hand to lead you around the dance floor. Let him show off how into you he is.

3. If he's in, you'll feel seen, special, desired, and worth it.

When I ask you to let him lead, I'm not trying to take you back to the 1950s. We women are powerful. When we set our intentions, we can cause almost anything to happen (including a relationship). But have you ever had the experience of having a kinda/sorta/mostly boyfriend who left you wondering once again, "Does he *like* like me? Or is he just going along for the sex?" Giving a man the chance to lead lets you see where he's leading you to as well as the pace at which he plans to get you there.

Now, I have a good friend who's a well-known matchmaker and she disagrees with me. She says she wouldn't be married to her husband if she didn't make all the moves. She continually makes the moves for their life together even today; he's slow to make decisions and the final call.

This was my experience with my (beloved) ex-husband as well. So if you don't mind being in charge, or you prefer calling all the shots, then go ahead and take the lead. When I was twenty-two, I wanted that control, but by the time I was in my thirties, I found it exhausting.

Now, when I say "let him lead" I don't mean sit back and make him do everything. As his dance partner, you're right there, ready to go when he takes your hand to dance. Men say over and over that they need encouragement. They appreciate after the first few dates if you start suggesting things and making dates too. That's partnership. They have a need to feel desired as well, so you want to do your part of partnership. When Dave said, "Weekends and Wednesdays are for Wendy," that let me know we were in the swing of things, and I started helping (even more) with the planning, since the dates were already set.

If you keep the pace from the beginning, you'll learn quickly how much he wants to make it happen with you. You'll see that he did the work to lay the foundation for your courtship (or not). Not so great to realize three months in that you're in this thing with him because he simply picked up the phone when you called or answered his door for you when you showed up at 10:45 PM.

Here's a tale of a man who showed great interest in words but did not back them up with actions.

Date #74
Smarty-Pants

Setting: Drinks at the Palace Hotel, San Francisco, CA

This one was smart, smart, smart—PhD-in-molecular-biophysics smart, graduated-from-Harvard smart, which should have been intimidating but for some reason wasn't.

He was cute and somewhat charmed by me (and my storytelling abilities) and had a couple of interesting stories himself.

We had a long date where the time just flew. There seemed to be a healthy balance of both of us doing the talking and listening. I appreciated his sense of humor and quirkiness. He explained how neutrons behave in the atomic nucleus, and in that moment he was totally sexy. And whether he knows he's doing it or not, he can give that look—you know, *that* look, the one that triggers a physical jolt throughout a woman's body.

We took a walk in the rain. As I ducked under his umbrella, he put his arm around my shoulders and it seemed to fit nicely. He made me feel safe and wanted. At the end of the date, I wished hard that he'd kiss me. I got my wish. As we parted, we were smitten, and we had a promised future date TBD.

So what happened?

I wanted to leave you with, "It was a long, drawn-out, terribly romantic mess that ended badly." But no, you deserve the truth, which is what this book is for.

Yummy date, yes? We emailed back and forth, and it was all exciting and promising. And then he attended a friend's wedding. He saw his ex-girlfriend there and, as he puts it, "against my better judgment, I got back together with her."

Okay, women. This is where you and I walk away. Which is what I did. I replied to his verbose, entertaining, and apologetic email, thanking him for such a kind, lengthy apology. I answered the many questions he'd asked me in his email. And I wished him the best of luck with his girlfriend. All done, yes? No, of course not.

He wrote back, this time asking more questions. I politely sent a response, because my mama raised me right. You don't want to be rude by not answering someone's questions. Before I knew it we were writing to each other short-story-length emails multiple times a day, his always filled with loads of questions for me to respond to. It was an emailing frenzy for nearly a month.

Eventually I caught on. I can be slow. I said, "Wait. We aren't friends. I can't date you. We need to stop writing right now. Go be happy with your girlfriend!"

But he wanted to be friends. He was insistent about it.

Here's a glaring warning: don't do what I did. I became his "friend," but I was secretly biding my time waiting for the volatile relationship with the "crazy girlfriend" that was never supposed to work out anyway to implode so I could swoop in, repair his heart, and save the day, providing him an awe-inspiring relationship with a sane person like he always wanted, where we all lived happily ever after. Of course, I was hoping for an implosion of said bad relationship sooner rather than later.

Guess what. It came. Later. Much, much, much, much, much later. And when it did, guess who he wasn't interested in dating anymore. Once he was single, I wasn't his type. I was crushed. I handled it badly. I felt stupid. I knew better. So do you. Don't be that girl.

When to Call It Quits If He's "Too Busy"

He says, "I'd like to see you again, but this week is crazy-busy." You wait. And wait. You might receive a call, an email, a text, and more details about how busy he is and how he wants to see you again.

If this is happening to you, I'm sorry. It's a drag. But it doesn't mean it's over. It means he's busy.

The true answer to the question, "Is he really busy?" is that you will be able to tell in time. Take him at his word and go live your life. Keep dating. If he comes back around, fantastic. If not, you didn't waste your time. Also, if he's in a time of his life where he truly is busy, like when he's building his company or balancing raising his children along with a packed work schedule and you need someone who is available for you often, please don't try to change him or his circumstances. You two simply may not be a good match. We'd all like to think that his being cute and a great kisser is all there is to it, but timing and a compatible lifestyle are key elements to living happily ever after.

Instead of asking, "Is he really busy?" try asking yourself, "How long am I willing to be driven insane, not getting the attention I need?" At some point you might need to quit or refocus for your own sanity.

34

When Should I Sleep with Him for the First Time?

"**When is the right time** to sleep with him for the first time so this turns into a long-term relationship?"

This is my number one most-asked sex question. Women are plagued, tortured, and run themselves ragged with this question.

Want to know the statement that usually follows that question?

"I slept with him too early, and now I don't know how I can recover this. I'm not sure he'll take me seriously or consider me for something long-lasting, since I gave it up too fast."

Well, here's some welcome news. Most men don't think like we do. Women tend to be strategic. If you read the previous section, you'll know my thoughts on being strategic when it comes to dating. We think the timing of the "when" will make or break the relationship. If we time it just right, everything else will fall into place and it will become the long-term relationship we hoped for.

I have listened to close to five hundred men of varying ages answer this very question. On the Sunday afternoon of the two-day sex workshop I lead for PAX Programs, we have a "man panel" Q&A discussion. In more than one hundred workshops, this specific question comes up every single time. Often the men are baffled by it.

They hear some version of the question, "When is the right time to have sex for the first time in a new relationship so it will lead to something lasting?" and they ask, "What does she mean by this?" or, "Is this a real question?" It's confusing to them because they know there's no such thing as a formulaic "right time." Most men aren't strategic about it like many women are. What can I say? Men are strange. Men think sex is just a fun thing to do with someone they like. Weird, I know. But when pressed for an answer, the majority of men say, "The right time to have sex for the first time is when we're both ready." That sounds all right to me.

One married man I interviewed said, "Back when I was dating, there were a couple of women I liked and wanted to pursue a relationship with, but they made me wait a long time for sex, so I broke up with them. They were putting me through the paces. I'm not going to marry someone if sex is treated like a prize at the end of an obstacle course. My wife doesn't hassle me about sex every time I want it and vice versa."

Sex is not a trading card. Men hate when they know the two of you are both ready but you're holding out for some sort of strategic reason.

How can you tell you're ready? When you know him and like him well enough that you want to stick around—because once you sleep with him and all the happy hormones like oxytocin and dopamine go coursing through your body, you're probably going to want to even more. First date, first week, first month, first year, on your wedding night: it's all good.

I know this upsets some women because our culture tells us that there's a "right way," and that that way is usually to wait it out—even if you're ready early. Many books are sold, many dating coaches are paid, and many matchmakers have specific, strategic rules that they promise will work, but there's no magic formula. If there were One True Way, we'd all know it by now. And guess what: I know a lot of women in long-term marriages who married the love of their life after having sex with him on the first date. I'm not advocating for sex on the first date across the board, but I'm here to say that I know it happens in the world, and sometimes—when it's meant to be—it works out just as well as if you wait.

Once people are married, society automatically legitimizes the relationship, and everyone around you can presume that you must have waited the appropriate amount of time because it worked out and there's a paper and a ring and a videotape of it somewhere to prove it. I wanted to know, so I went straight to the source. I used Survey Monkey to interview more than one hundred married people. I started my survey with the question, "On a scale of one to ten, ten being extremely happy, one being miserable, how happily married are you?" Anyone who ranked below a seven was excluded from my study.

Next I asked one hundred happily married people the question, "How many dates had you been on before you had sex with your partner?"

- 20 percent said first date
- 35 percent had sex by their third date
- 53 percent had sex by their fifth date
- 76 percent had sex by the time they'd reached a dozen dates

When I interviewed men about sex on the first date, they were all over the map. At the start of my research I thought it was generational. The fifty-year-old didn't respect a woman who would do that, and the twenty-five-year-old guy was cool about it. But as more and more men spoke up, I could see it's not generational; it simply varies from man to man, just like it varies from woman to woman. I've heard from plenty of older men who say it makes no difference; in fact, most of their girlfriends (and wives) had had sex on the first date. I've also heard men in their twenties say they would not consider her as long-term-relationship potential if she had sex on the first date. All in all, roughly 80 percent of the men say it makes no difference when they sleep with a woman for the first time. Even sex on the first night would not be the make-or-break thing. And all men said that (unless the sex was beyond bad) it is never the sex that ends it; it's something else about the dynamic of the pair that's the showstopper.

As we touched on earlier, women are driven to time sex just right, like a formula for dating success. If it's too soon, you're a slut. Too late, he'll think you're frigid and lose interest. Or if we wait too long and they go away, they won't ever know how good we are in bed, which would have sealed the deal. There's no winning the strategy game when it comes to sex.

You might find yourself in the "too early" camp because, well, he looks so yummy. Immediately afterward your inner critic beats you up for blowing it. She tells you, you were too easy and you've lost all the power since you've put your biggest gambling chip on the table: the sex chip. He wanted it. You gave it up. Now you have nothing left for bargaining. You fear he's gone, because sex was all he wanted anyway, probably. (Raise your hand if you know what I'm talking about.)

You call your dating buddy for reassurance—reassurance that you're amazing enough that he'll call you again once you've had sex with him. And you wait. And you think of him constantly. And you know exactly how long 259,200 seconds feels in a 72-hour period. You plot and wonder how you can reel him back. How can I make him take me seriously? How can I be my influential, powerful, and respected self now?

If you've ever had this experience, you're in good company. You're loved and surrounded by thousands if not millions of your sisters just like you.

If you want to help prevent this in the future, you can try a few things.

1. Be sure you know him well enough to have some level of the commitment you're both looking for figured out prior to having sex. This will help you both avoid the situation described above.
2. Before you have sex for the first time, let him know this is a vulnerable time for you and what you need is for him to call you the next morning—or later in the day if he spends the night. Having a future date on the books that isn't too far out also helps.

These things will help, but nothing is foolproof. I think this is why Chunky Monkey was invented.

It bears repeating that I'm not advocating having sex on the first date. It could do you crazy kids some good to spend time together to get to know each other. You might find out if you actually like him. That said, I know many married couples who did have sex on the first date, and hey, look, they're married! I know a woman who was out with a group of friends and met a man. It was a bit of an impromptu blind date. They hit it off so much so that she had sex with him that night in the back of a moving vehicle. They've been married for more than ten years, have two beautiful kids, and are pillars of their community. Another married woman I know hadn't seen or even talked to an old high school friend in thirty years. She meant to meet him for a cup of coffee at his place for a catch-up session and instead ended up with some sugar in his bed. She's still in it—permanently. (Not to worry; he does let her out of it for several hours a day.)

Here's further evidence that sleeping with someone on a first date actually can work out, even if you don't end up with your happily ever after: my Date #1.

Date #1
My First

Setting: Drinks at the Swiss Hotel, Sonoma, CA

Date #1 was a completely unintentional one on my part. My girl-friend Clare asked me out for drinks, and en route her friend rang her cell to ask if he could join. He knew I would be there and, unbe-knownst to me, had been devising a way to put himself in front of me.

Two weeks prior to this fateful night, he and I met for the first time at Steiner's, the largest bar in town that caters to the local work-ing class, young jocks, and mediocre pool players. He sat next to me at the bar while Clare took her turn at the pool table. She and I were playing doubles and losing badly. He extended his hand. "I'm James, friend of Clare's."

I took it, our light gray-blue eyes met with recognition of old souls meeting again, and in that moment, I abandoned my beloved friend, leaving her to the pool sharks. His smile was broad, our con-versation animated. I suppose that's what people call a "spark." It was the kind that made my body shiver and my mind plot out ways to win him over. He was gorgeous and rugged; Irish (my weakness); six-foot-one and slender with a magical and elusive charm so thick I knew I was had. He seemed too amazing to be true.

This night, Clare and I grabbed the last available table at the Swiss Hotel, cozying in underneath a red heat lamp that was crack-ling and cranking on high though still unable to do the proper job required to keep us comfortable on this chilly fall night. Red wine was the only choice; a cocktail or white would freeze our hands.

"The Swiss," as locals call it, is the nighttime spot to chat with your neighbors over a refreshing adult beverage. Sure, they serve food, and it's pretty damned good, but out front you'll mostly see drinks—a lot of them. The lively conversation between neighboring tables is one of the best parts of living in a small country town. You'll find vintners sharing their wine with realtors, bed-and-breakfast owners, and politicians any night of the week.

Within moments, Date #1 joined us, ordered his Glariffee (the house coffee drink with many secret ingredients) and got right to work. His efforts to catch my attention were thwarted as two other men joined us. (Did I mention that Clare is stunningly beautiful and has a lovely Irish accent?) One guy was from England; the other from Germany. Competition forced him to raise his game with a pitch so obvious to everyone that he wanted to be on a date with me that eventually Clare couldn't take it anymore. She downed her nearly three-quarters-full glass of wine in one gulp and slammed it down empty with such force on the wooden table I was certain she'd crack the stem. She giggled, winked at me, grinned widely, and in her most dramatic, fake-mad tone exclaimed, "Wellllll . . . you two, I think you need some time alone. I'm outta here." She rose, kicked her chair back under the table for effect, and turned to leave, and directly behind her cute, skinny Irish frame went Mr. Germany and Mr. England.

So what happened?

This impromptu date lasted sixteen hours, was one of the most significant nights of my life, and led to a long-term relationship (a little more than a year) until he left the United States for his homeland. This was a case of bad timing. We were both recently divorced and he just couldn't commit (a sample case of the newly divorced man—and woman, in this case). I wasn't willing to chuck my life to live in a foreign country without knowing if he could ever commit to me. Years later we both felt regret, but we'd also both moved on. He was, and will remain, one of the great loves of my life. Just because you don't end up with someone who means something to you doesn't mean that the experience wasn't important—sometimes even life-changing.

35

Let's Talk About Sex

Let's do it, let's talk about sex. Or, more accurately, let's talk more about sex, since we've talked about it already. After you've been dating awhile, it's going to come up (no pun intended), so it's best to be prepared when it does. Here are a few of the topics that have come up time and again both for me and for countless women I've known when sex is on the menu.

How to Course-Correct If You Went Too Far

What do you do if you went further with him than you'd intended to? How do you pull it back?

You tell him; you open up your mouth and tell him.

You'll feel vulnerable; that's a positive thing. It might look like this:

"So the other night . . . I didn't intend for us to do anything other than watch that action film. Maybe do some kissing during the chase scenes; that's it. I kind of got ahead of myself there. You looked so sexy. I know we've already had sex, but I'm not quite ready to be in a sexual relationship yet. Do you mind if we wait a little longer so I can get to know you before we do that again?"

How Much Is Too Much to Say about Your Past?

How much should you tell him about you past? The answer is it's different for different men. It used to be that by and large, men didn't want to know. In the 1997 film *Chasing Amy*, Ben Affleck's character was driven mad once he learned of his girlfriend's sexual history. That was the entire plot. If the man you are dating is in love with you, he may not want to know these details. It may drive him nuts.

When some men ask, they truly want to know. For some, it's a turn-on. It's an enhancement to your intimate relationship. This is more the exception than the rule. I listened to fifty men speak on this topic when I was conducting one-on-one social research in the fall of 2012. Prior to my research I had assumptions, and, boy, was I wrong. Here's what these men taught me:

Inaccurate assumption #1: This craving for sexual detail is generational. Older men don't want to know and younger men do want to know.

Nope. I was shocked at how many men in their fifties and sixties wanted to know their wife's history because they thought it was hot. On the other hand, there were some men in their early twenties who didn't want to know anything about their girlfriend's history because they wanted to think of her as pure. (Sigh.)

Inaccurate assumption #2: This craving for sexual detail is only the territory of very sexually experienced men.

Nope. I spoke to men I've known for more than twenty-five years, and they have very—and I do mean very (and varied)—active sex lives. You might consider them "sexperts." These men love women and want to know as many as they can intimately but did not want the details or history of the women they had sex with. Compare this with a man who'd only been with two women in his fifty-plus years and greatly enjoyed hearing the sexcapades in his wife's history.

Inaccurate assumption #3: This craving for sexual detail is only wanted if the relationship is only sexual in nature.

Nope. Wanting to know—or not wanting to know—your sexual history has everything to do with men's fantasies of you. For some men, details enhance your sexuality and desirability. For other men, thinking they might be the only one who's ever had sex with you is the ultimate fantasy.

Know your audience. If he asks you about your sexual history, you may want to do a little investigative work before you launch into the stories. Ask some clarifying questions such as:

"Are you asking about my sexual history because knowing about my past would be a turn-on?"

"Are you asking me about my sexual history because you'd like to know my preferences?"

And even if he wants the details because it would enhance his fantasy of you, that doesn't mean you have to provide them. If it makes you uncomfortable or doesn't sit right with you, you don't have to. Your private history is just that: private and history.

For me personally, I didn't like to risk it. Given that I was married for twelve years, I assumed my sexual partner(s) knew I'd had sex with my husband. That's how I played it until I met #121. Dave was disappointed when I didn't initially open up. He felt we were missing out on fun, intimate storytelling opportunities. As I got to know him, I realized he's not at all a jealous person, and he really did want to know my past, not necessarily for my sexual preferences but more for the adventures and the overall sexual expression of who I am. I'm happy to say that he likes and respects me even more now that he's heard the stories (as many as I can remember, anyway) and has a full picture of who I am. Dave is exceptional, but I also believe he's an exception-man when it comes to talking about sexual history.

If a man is asking with the goal of figuring out what you like, you can tell him if you're comfortable doing so. And you can speak about it while keeping the past in the past. Don't say, "I love to have sex doggie style," or, "My favorite position is doggie style." Either statement might have him picturing you posed in doggie style with a conga line of men behind you. Instead, you could say, "Let's do doggie style," keeping it in the present and between the two of you. Once you've done that with him, you can always refer to it as, "I love when we do doggie style."

You can say, "Let's try_____," with whatever it is. But be warned, if you say, "Let's try . . . ," he might assume you've never tried it before. It might be kind of weird if you say, "Let's try missionary position" (unless you actually haven't ever done it missionary).

Often, men don't ask about a woman's history. Again, your sexual history is yours. You don't need to share it. Unless . . .

How to Tell Your Date You Have a Sexually Transmitted Infection

If you have a sexually transmitted infection, especially a chronic one like herpes, you need to tell your partner when you know the relationship is turning sexual. You don't have to reveal it on the first date, but when the kissing turns to more than a good-night kiss at the door, it's time. Pick a time when you're not in the middle of a heavy make-out session. Neither one of you will have all your faculties and won't have full choice or consent in the matter.

Make the time a special date like a brunch or barbeque at your house. Somewhere private where you can speak freely and if need be you both can deal with any emotion without outside interference. Speak about it calmly, like you were saying, "I have green eyes." There's no upside to adding drama or backstory. Know the details of your STI, how you're treating it, what the odds are of contracting it, and how you plan to help protect him from contracting it. Be ready for questions.

The hardest part of all is granting him space to think about it, to research it, and to decide. This is a vulnerable time for you. You'll want reassurance from him that it will be okay and that he'll stay with you, but this is not the time to lean in. Provide space.

I helped a woman go through the process of informing partners she had herpes. When she realized she had it, she also learned she'd had it for a number of years—and was utterly horrified. She'd been with several men in the time she was unknowingly positive. She collected herself, sat down with her telephone, and one by one, made the calls to men she'd been intimate with to let them know she may have inadvertently exposed them. Every man she talked with was kind and thanked her for the information.

Then something stunning happened: nearly every man she talked to said, "Hey, so the next time you're in town, we should get together." Meaning sex. We were shocked. As women, we realized that neither of us would ever have said, "Let's get together again" for sex after this sort of bomb was dropped. Risk exposure? It would take a crowbar to pry our inner thighs open.

For days I thought about what seemed to be this significant difference between men and women, and I came to a conclusion: while at first this situation seemed to be one of personal safety or lack thereof (with women being more protective of their bodies than men), I don't believe that it is. Women can be as reckless with their sexual health as men and vice versa, but a woman's inner critic is generally more focused on (unattainable) perfection than a man's. A dude with an STI? According to our inner critic, having sex with him could make us damaged goods and not worth the risk. The inner critic in most men won't strive for that crazy-making level of unattainable perfection, making men more willing to look past that for true love.

Bottom line: sisters, let's work on taking good care of our health, on being as safe as possible, and on not shaming or jumping to conclusions where STIs—and the people who have or have had them, including ourselves—are concerned. Nothing in life—driving, crossing the street, relationships—is risk-free, and the joy happens in the balance between being safe and having a blast.

Fetishes, Kinks, and Preferences

If you have a fetish, a kink, a preference, or just something you really love, most men are excited to have this information. A man wants to give you pleasure, and he thinks it's a kindness if you share what feels good to you with him. If your body is different or works in unexpected ways, this is all information worthy of sharing.

One man said, "We are way more kinky than women are. You just don't hear us talking about it because we don't want to be disrespectful and freak you out." So if you have something you like that's a bit afield, chances are it's going to be welcome news to him. Three cheers for more variety!

As Dan Savage (sex columnist, gay activist, and my personal hero) says, "There's something the straights can learn from the gays, and that's the phrase 'What are you into?'" You could share these preferences up front if you have the type of guy on your hands who wants to hear it. Or you can let these preferences unfold naturally as your relationship deepens. There's no right or wrong way. You could ask, "How would you best like to get to know me intimately? Would you like to talk about it, or should we just see what happens?"

When you do share with him your kinks, preferences, or whatever makes you unique, don't make it a downer—it's not a problem. Instead, be enthusiastic. This is excellent news! One, he gets to have sex with you, and two, as a part of that super-fun package he gets to know a part of you that's probably integral to your sense of self. That's a privilege.

If you're someone who has a strong sexual preference or two, I recommend you state your case up front—preferably as soon as the relationship turns sexual. This will help you sort quickly. Never forget that there are people out there who want you to have your heart's desire and will be more than happy to help provide it.

36

Friends with Benefits and Nontraditional Arrangements

Say you're still dating, but you've hit a dry spell. A really, really dry spell. One of the hardest and sometimes most frustrating things about being single is that there's no partner to fulfill your sexual needs and desires. And while masturbation with toys will do in a pinch, let's face it: solo play doesn't come anywhere near what is possible when you're in yummy entanglement with a mate. This section is designed to help you have what you need when you're living the single lifestyle while still searching for your lasting partner.

Friends with benefits (FWB) is a popular one, so we'll start there. I'll share what I've learned, how it works, for whom it could work, and the pitfalls to avoid.

Who You Need to Be

Grabbing a FWB partner is not for everyone. The type of woman who thrives with a FWB arrangement is in sync with the following points:

- **She can actually do it.** I mean, really, you have to be the type of woman who can do this. Not all women can, in light of their religious, spiritual, and personal beliefs. I wouldn't recommend trying a FWB relationship if it's in direct conflict with your integrity, spirituality, or soul or if it causes you to have opinions and judgments that are negative toward yourself or toward people who do this.

- **She can compartmentalize.** You need the ability to put this relationship in a box of its own before it starts. Separate it from any romantic notion that you two will get together and live happily ever after.

- **She is willing to forgo a long-term relationship.** I believe this is one of the longest, hardest lessons I learned in a decade of dating. In the ten years I was single and looking for my partner, I always had a friend with benefits. I was masterful at compartmentalizing, and understanding that my friend and I had no future. And I think it's why I was single so long. What I say here isn't the one and only truth but rather my point of view based on my experience and the experiences of my clients.

    If you're not ready for or are not interested in having a full-time romantic relationship, a FWB scenario might be an excellent alternative. If you're ready to be in a committed relationship, I don't recommend trying a FWB if you see each other often (like once a week) as it may get in the way of you being free to meet someone for something deeper. No matter how much dating you're doing outside of this arrangement, no matter how much of an expert you think you are at this (and I'm saying this from experience), there's not enough of a gap for a full-time partner to come in. A part of your heart is not completely free to available suitors because it belongs to your friend. While seeing your FWB you will tend to attract daters who are not interested in or ready for a relationship or those who are polyamorous or prefer open relationships. (More on them in a bit.)

- **She is open and free in her sexuality.** You will need to communicate about things that can be uncomfortable or painful to talk about with your FWB—things that may be allowed more time and space to ease into in a conventional relationship but that are best addressed sooner rather than later in a FWB situation.

- **She is communicative.** You'll need the skills of negotiating your FWB deal up front, and you'll need to be able to distinguish what you need without compromising yourself along the way. Set limits to maintain enough distance to not be too disappointed when the FWB arrangement ends.

- **She has support.** You have a best friend or dating ally. Is this person comfortable listening to you talk about your FWB? If so, fill him or her in. Are things getting too intense with your FWB? The opposite? Be honest with your support person and with yourself.

- **She is willing to fall in love with him.** When you have sex with a person consistently for an extended period of time, no matter how well you picked, no matter how well you compartmentalize, no matter how well you communicate, the possibility of falling in love is ever present. This could end up hurting down the line, so you have to be willing to deal with the potential heartache.

- **She is willing for it to end.** It's a friends-with-benefits situation; it's not a relationship. This is not to say it can never turn into a relationship if it's something you both want; however, many women make the mistake of thinking this is a shortcut into a relationship with a man who says he doesn't want a relationship (with you). Don't be your own best con artist—95 percent of the time it doesn't turn into that dream relationship you'd secretly hoped for. Don't sell yourself out in hopes of being in that elusive 5 percent.

The way I see it, there are three categories you might pick from for a FWB. Only you can decide what ends up working best for you.

Category #1: Someone You Love

The first time I entered into a FWB relationship, I picked someone I loved—and wanted a relationship with. I thought I'd shortcut the route to girlfriend even though he told me, "I'm quite fond of you, but I will never fall in love with you." Ouch.

This FWB relationship lasted four and a half years. I ended it. We could have gone on the rest of our lives, and I would have gone the rest of mine compromised and not getting what I needed in a partner. Thankfully, we are still close friends who love and care about each other deeply even today.

Date #4
The Man in Black

Setting: Drinks at Murphy's Irish Pub, Sonoma, CA

Date #4 was another unintentional date; that happens when you live in a town so small you know everyone within five minutes of arriving with your U-Haul.

I'd had my eye on him for years. I'd watch him around town and enjoyed the view from afar. He was spectacularly my type: black leather jacket, simple black T-shirt, and black jeans. He looked like an artist, an actor, a tortured musician, or possibly Lou Reed's best friend. Someone who would have run with the New York Dolls circa

1972, living in clubs like CBGB and Max's Kansas City. He had that heroin-chic look, a tall, dark, and handsomely aging bad boy. Needless to say, this is not a typical look for the men of the Sonoma wine country. Also needless to say, I took notice.

There he was again, sitting at a small wooden table under the large green awning of the local pub, his pint of Bitburger still and lifeless, his Marlboro smoldering in a heaping-full ashtray, his hand moving fast and furious with a cheap Bic pen on yellow index cards scattered everywhere.

I stumbled around to find my own empty table, pint in one hand and an only marginally interesting book in the other. All the tables were full.

"Come join me," he said as he met my eyes.

(Thank you, baby Jesus.)

Somehow I had finagled my way to his table. Miraculous. Okay, maybe not so miraculous. I'm crafty that way. And let's not forget, it took me more than two years to get that seat.

Six hours—we talked at that little wooden table for six hours. He told me his whole life story, and as it turns out, he was indeed his projected persona, New York Dolls and all.

So what happened?

The first date ended up lasting twenty hours. We continued talking (among other activities) for more than four years. He taught me things about myself and my sexuality I will forever be grateful for.

Category #2: Someone Unavailable for a Relationship or Uninterested in One

When it comes to relationships, timing is half the battle. And sometimes you'll run into a great match for you but at the wrong time for him. He might be emotionally unavailable or uninterested in a relationship for a variety of reasons, the most common of which is that he is newly divorced. Or he might be unavailable because raising children or building a business before committing to a romantic partner is the priority.

Then there are those who just aren't interested in a monogamous relationship. They'll tell you that, and it's your job to take it at face value.

My second FWB relationship was with someone who was unavailable for the type of relationship I was looking for. This FWB plan lasted several years. Again, we're still friends who love and care about each other deeply.

Date #39
Sheer Will

Setting: Drinks at Front Room at the Wharf, Vallejo, CA

Mr. Tall, Handsome, and Newly Divorced arrived right when I did. Sexual attraction was not going to be a problem. His intensity was more than enough for both of us, and he was fixed on me.

Not five minutes into settling in, he exclaimed, "I won't ever be monogamous again. I'd like to have more than one partner now that my marriage is over. That 'one woman until death do us part' thing didn't work for me."

"How many partners do you need?" I asked in a curious, non-threatening tone.

He looked at me, seemingly stunned that I would even ask this.

I continued, "If you could have everything you needed, including the variety and frequency, how many women would it take?"

He sat silent, so I did too. More than a minute had passed when he said, "Four. Four would do it."

"You have to be the main one. You're going to be in charge of the other three. This was your idea!" he exclaimed.

We had a delightful time enjoying cocktails and designing an alternate universe for him.

So what happened?

I said yes to another date. And then another one. And then another. But I knew in my heart of hearts running his house with three other women living in it was not my destiny.

Category #3: Someone Incompatible for a Long-Term Relationship

My third FWB relationship lasted more than two years. On our second date, I said, "I really like you. I'm a big fan of yours, but we have no long-term future. Do you still want to be friends—I mean, really be friends?" I said this because I'd learned enough about him in two dates to know that we were incompatible for the long haul. But I liked the type of person he was—namely, amazing.

The FWB plan worked well with him. Like the other two, we are still close friends who love and care about each other.

|||| |||| ||||

Did you notice the one common thread shared by each man? We're still close friends who love and care about each other deeply. One possibility to strive for is being friends. You know, honest-to-God real friends. Even when the sex ends, you two can be good together. You can love and care about each other even after the benefits part is complete. You don't have to set it up that way, but that's the way it has worked out for me. It might have something to do with the fact that I sleep with people I like as people. Call me crazy.

So let's review: What can you expect from a FWB scenario?

- That you might not find a long-term relationship during this phase.
- To do some deal-making so you get your needs met.
- Hot sex.
- Happy, sexy hormones—and the delusions that come with them.
- For it to end—possibly before you're ready.

What Are Some Alternatives to Friends with Benefits?

I collaborated with a dozen sister-girlfriends to give you the pros and cons to each of the five following alternatives to FWB scenarios. Let's start with abstinence and work our way up.

- **Celibacy:** Some women can pull it off; some can't. Some are empowered by it and, with a few toys thrown in, satisfied, while others feel a loss of self and the shutting down of their sensuality. The upside is you're safe from STIs. The downside, whether you're empowered or annoyed by celibacy, you're at risk for disconnecting from your own sensuality. Get what you need to take care of yourself. Do things to stay in your body such as dance, yoga, working out, going on nature walks, getting a massage, taking bubble baths, and masturbating. You might consider incorporating sex toys into your routine (if you don't already) to keep yourself feeling sexy, relieved, and healthy.

- **Occasional flings:** The upsides include getting your sexual needs met, experiencing variety, and having exciting adventures. The downsides include possibly contracting sexually transmitted infections; putting yourself in compromising positions with strangers where you may not be able to clearly state your needs and boundaries; risk of general safety; potential awkwardness; and lack of intimacy and connection.

- **Third party:** You may enjoy stepping into an arrangement where you're the third person, usually with a man and woman in an established couple. Congratulations! You are known in various swinger, polyamorous, and sex-positive communities as a "unicorn"— you're that rare. The upside: you'll be in high demand, so you'll have the luxury of being selective. On the downside, it is emotionally overwhelming for some women. Finding yourself alone at the end of a play session as the two of them stroll off toward home hand in hand can be a bit of an unexpected punch to the gut.

- **Multiple partners:** Multiple partners may give you the freedom of not becoming as attached as you would to one primary friends-with-benefits deal. Plus you'll have variety. However, this scenario has the potential to be confusing and sometimes emotionally overwhelming. You may be with one while longing for the other, or for the long-term partner you've not yet met.

Polyamory and Open Relationships

Polyamory can be defined as having more than one romantic relationship at a time where everyone involved not only knows about the relationships but consents to them. The term "open relationship" can be used in a broader sense to include polyamorous relationships as well as consenting affairs, play partners, trysts, friends with benefits and any other random arrangement one would like to toss in. The term "monogamish" (coined by my "boyfriend," Dan Savage) describes couples who are mostly monogamous, present that way socially, and from time to time get the hall pass—whatever that looks like for them. Each of these categories have one thing in common: the people involved aren't cheating on their partner. Everyone is on the same page and has made consenting deals to be happy in this type of relationship (or at least that's what the goal and hope is, anyway).

As our culture steps further and further away from that 1950s conventional deal where a man and a woman marry, he works to put a roof over their head, and she stays at home to raise the children, people are getting creative out there. It's fascinating, the deals we can make with each other in partnership(s) to get our needs met. Some want a traditional life, while others want more of a fifty-fifty partnership that has come to be prevalent in the last thirty years. Most relationships require monogamy, but an increasing number are considering "monogamish" or open, polyamorous (poly) relationships.

A poly relationship is, in fact, a real relationship. You're in a relationship that includes all the fixings of a monogamous one—affection, sex, and emotional support—only you'll be sharing these things with the other partners in your equation as well. Polyamory is a balancing act like any other kind of relationship, and the key to successful poly partnerships is the same key to most monogamous ones: communication. If you think a poly arrangement might be right for you, read a book or two on the subject and go for it. But remember to check in with yourself along the way and ask if this is what you really want and need.

Also worth noting: if you're coming into an already existing relationship as a permanent play partner or a partner who's not primary, be sure you are getting what you need. Just because you're not primary doesn't mean that what you need counts any less.

The most important part of any relationship (monogamous or not) is that it works for everyone involved—that all are getting their needs met and nobody's doing it just to get along. Open and poly relationships work for some women. Keep in mind that, as in a friends-with-benefits package, you'll fill up your dating space with your partner(s) and will be less likely to find a monogamous mate, if that's what you crave.

You may have a preconceived notion about the person you're entering into a relationship with, such as if he met the right girl (you) he wouldn't need more than one partner. Don't kid yourself. Men and women in these types of relationships understand themselves. They need a variety of partners and they know it. You're not going to be so special or talented that he'll need no one else. Don't try to flip this one to monogamy. I've seen the results, and it doesn't end well for anyone. If monogamy is what you need, look elsewhere.

卌   卌   卌

After your first few dates (or your first few dozen), you'll learn quite a bit about dating, what you are looking for, and what you have to offer. You also might find yourself confused, frustrated, or approaching burnout. Sure, you've had some good dates, but then there are the ones you could have skipped entirely. Setting boundaries and being gracious isn't easy, and gaining confidence around this whole process doesn't happen overnight. The urge to get a little too interested in that one guy didn't go away just because you deemed him not worth your time, and your inner critic is giving you a run for your money at every turn. You might hit a rough patch or a dry spell along the way, but because you're you, you dust yourself off, rehydrate, and keep going.

When it gets rough, remember to pull back and take care of yourself along the way—whether that means taking a break from dating, taking part in self-care, or exploring how to have your needs met while you're still searching for your partner or partners. This in turn will not only help you take care of yourself but it will also help you continue to put your best foot forward each time you step out to meet your potential mate, bringing you ever closer to your very own version of happily ever after.

Conclusion:
Happily Ever After (Really!)

"Happily ever after" is what most of us are going for. Many women have ideas about what we deserve—I mean, after all, we were promised our very own version of a handsome prince and a fairy-tale ending, or at least that's how it felt when we were little. We saw *Snow White and the Seven Dwarfs* and *Cinderella* and we knew what was coming. He's tall, has a full head of hair, and a big horse, and he's going to ride up and save us from a boring life alone. We'll stand at an altar decorated with a canopy of white roses in front of our friends, family, and fairy godmother, and he'll promise to love us forever while we look pretty in our poofy white dress; and from that perfect moment on, nothing will ever change—ever.

I'm sure I don't need to tell you that the fairy-tale ending is just that: a fairy tale. It can be a big old setup for failure and heartache—for you, for him, for everyone. After all, that promise at the alter doesn't exactly guarantee you a 100 percent chance of staying together, and even if you do, that doesn't mean everyone who stays married is happy.

Now, I'm not saying run screaming in the other direction, and I don't want to rain on the parades of women who want a fairy-tale wedding and a Disneyesque happily-ever-after. If you want it, go get it! What I do want to do as we near the end of our trip together is to look at what you can do to boost your odds to be truly happy once you find the right person for you, the one you want to spend the rest of your days with and who wants to do the same with you.

As you're dating, sorting, and letting him lead (to see where he's leading you), you're learning about him. Does he have enough of what you need? Does he check the boxes on the important things that matter to your life? Go back to that list you made. How's he doing? As you're assessing if you're a good fit for each other, pay attention to one thing and one thing only: substance.

As your relationship grows, do the two of you continue to give each other enough of what you need? How's your communication style? Does it match? Does he see you? Is he able to make you happy? Are you your best self with him? Are you empowered? Are you fully self-expressed? Do your friends like who you are now that you're with him? Or has he changed you into some contorted, strange version of someone who kinda looks like you?

Pay attention to the substance, not just the feelings, because feelings can be fleeting and changeable. As you're falling in love with him, you might find yourself singing the Beatles song "All You Need Is Love." It's a catchy song, but I wouldn't base my entire life on the lyrics, because, sister, you have needs beyond love, and that first year, you're going to be in the love bubble. Make sure the things you need—the things that really matter to you—will be fulfilled with the deals you make in your partnership. And pay attention to how well you can make such deals with your partner.

As we move further and further away from marriage as a (traditional) necessity, we're able to step into marriages and relationships based on enhancing our lives and making our relationships deep and lasting for today's world. In doing so, people are choosing to make all kinds of different deals. Dave and I chose to have a private commitment ceremony with a dear friend officiating and four friends as witnesses. The ceremony had a personal meaning for us, which is why we didn't choose a traditional marriage (which didn't).

Many people, especially if they've been married before, decide marriage isn't for them. But does this mean their relationship is less valid or committed because of it? Paying attention to the substance instead of the form it takes gives you a chance to have a relationship by design. To be thoughtful while you work on what's important to both of you, instead of blindly taking the next expected cultural step. Do I have anything against marriage? Nope. Do I have anything against people choosing something other than marriage? Nope. I recommend you consider what it means to you and what type of union makes sense for you and your partner.

Once you've aligned on what works for both of you, don't let the pressures of society, family, or friends talk you out of what's best for you. I know plenty of people who are intentionally living together and intentionally not living together in beautiful, loving, connected marriages and partnerships. For example, I know a couple in San Francisco in their mid sixties who have been together for forty years and have maintained their own apartments one block from each other. Who's to question forty years of bliss?

Whether you decide to live a monogamous white-picket-fence life or have an open marriage while living side by side in a duplex, it's your choice to make. Who works, him or you or both? Are you two paying everything fifty-fifty? Will there be children or no children? Will he be the stay-at-home dad while you're the breadwinner? All good. I know of happy, committed relationships of all sorts and have seen everything I've just listed work well for years on end. This is what's possible when we're choosing partnership, instead of what our grandparents did, which was taking a wife or husband because that's what was expected and needed for survival.

The key to your happily-ever-after is living the life you want with the partner (or partners) that match you and your needs well. When everyone involved thinks they got the better end of the deal? That's what a true happily-ever-after looks like.

IHL   IHL   IHL

Well, gorgeous sister of mine, we've had an amazing journey together. I hope you're kicking back, relaxing in your yoga pants, and feeling proud of how far you've come since you opened the front cover of this little book.

As you continue to navigate the sometimes smooth, sometimes rocky seas of the dating life, know that I'm thinking of you. I'm keeping an eye out for you every time you step out the door on your next date. I'm rooting for you. He's out there, and he's on his way to you. He's going to love you for exactly who you are and exactly who you are not. He'll buy into that whole delicious package that is you, and you'll know this whole process was fully worth it (while sometimes being a total pain in the ass). I wish you all the luck, ease, and grace in finding your happiness.

Ready for my happily-ever-after?

Date #121
Date #1 Meets Date #121—
The Deus Ex Machina

Setting: Iced tea at Zuni, San Francisco, CA

"What about Thursday? I have ninety minutes in the evening," he said over email.

"Thursday? I can meet for a quick drink from 7 to 7:30. Are you willing to have such a short first date? It looks like our schedules are ridiculous, and I'm leaving for Mexico on Saturday." I replied to this cute engineer-by-day/musician-by-night. This may be my shortest email thread on record. I wrote him. He responded with gusto, and twenty-four hours later we'd set a date.

"Where do you want to meet?" he asked.

"Zuni." I picked Zuni as it was a block from where I was heading after our rushed date and because it's where the fancy people go, and I like fancy people.

"Zuni? Can I make an alternate suggestion? It's Tops is more my style," he responded.

Zuni not his style? A diner is more his style? In San Francisco? *Don't be judgy. Don't be judgy. Don't be judgy. Meet him first and then you can judge.* I put my fingers back on the keyboard and replied, "It's Tops it is. I'll see you there at seven."

Ten minutes before our scheduled date my text message dinged. "It's Tops is closed. I'll meet you at Zuni." (Thank you, restaurant gods.)

I charged into the restaurant five minutes late, nearly throwing my keys at the valet, as I knew my tardiness was cutting into our already too-short date. At the host station, I looked around the crowded bar area and spotted a tall, handsome man in a long, black coat and hat moving toward me. He leaned to my left side and his deep voice spoke softly into my ear, "There you are. I'd recognize you anywhere."

I shuddered. He was sexy, handsome, and smiling broadly. Instantly I recalled a line I once read in an article: "He looked like he could fuck me through a wall." Yep, this applies here. I knew I was sunk.

Before I could respond, our maître d' approached us, and we were shown to a two-top in the far corner.

"What's good here?" he asked.

"The burger is legendary. Once named best in the city, says Michael Bauer," I replied.

When the server appeared, Date #121 ordered the burger.

"We don't serve the burger at this hour. We serve it for lunch and after eleven," our server replied, with a hint of superiority in his tone.

Date #121 made a quick secondary choice and then went straight to the business of teasing me for inviting him to a place known for food they aren't willing to serve during their dinner hour.

In our limited time together, we managed to slip in key information about each other, like I was his first date in more than twenty-five years. I revealed he was my first date 100-and-something.

Next up, religion: we were both brought up in "kooky" ones. I regaled him with tales of my many attempts at getting excommunicated from the Mormon Church, culminating in my final (and successful) attempt, which took six months to complete.

We were both running late and didn't want to leave each other.

"Can I walk you to your reading?" he asked.

"Yes."

As we strolled, him on the outside of the sidewalk, me safely tucked on the inside, arm in arm, he took me nearly to the door of the venue when I stopped him, "Wait. We should say good-bye right here."

"Um, okay," he said curiously.

"Yeah, well, see that man about a hundred yards away? That's my ex-husband. You don't want to meet him right now, right?" I smiled awkwardly.

"Right. Good call." He beamed at me and gave a quick kiss good-bye, and he was gone.

                    ‖‖   ‖‖   ‖‖

So what happened?

Our second date lasted more than six hours. We fell in love with each other on this date.

Shortly after we started dating he confessed that he was certain I was sent to him. Every time he'd mention it, I would brush off the comment. We're both spiritual but not religious. He was certain it was fate, the goddess, spirit, the Universe, something bigger than we are that brought us together.

"Yeah, yeah, yeah . . . ," I thought.

Four months into our relationship I made a comment about a man we knew. "I wouldn't have dated that guy. He's too suburban for me. I like the urban guy."

Date #121 laughed right at me.

"What?" I asked.

"Um, you wrote to me online when I lived in San Jose."

"Yes, but your profile said San Francisco was your home," I said.

"No, it didn't. It said San Jose." He grinned widely and waited for it to compute.

"That's impossible. My OkCupid date radius was set for no more than twenty-five miles from Oakland. San Jose is well over fifty miles."

"I know," he said with the devilish grin I love so much.

He continued, "I know you well now. I know you never would have responded to my profile. I told you, the goddess brought you to me. Read it."

He opened up his old OkCupid profile on his cell phone and handed it to me. The first line read, "I am recently separated, and all about exploring my newfound freedom." I continued reading all the way through the profile and down to the bottom of the page called "I'm looking for," and the drop-down categories he chose were "new friends" and "short-term dating."

By the time I hit those final words, tears were streaming down my face. When my eyes met his, he was patiently waiting, looking at me intently, lovingly. He said, "I know. I told you so. The goddess brought you to me. Not only was I not in your search algorithm but I know you well enough now to know you never would have written to me."

I don't know how it happened. I really don't. I remember his profile being simple, direct, and bold; and beyond his good looks, I liked him on sight. I recognized him as being in my tribe. But how I even made it past the first sentence is a mystery and an act of something greater than myself.

|||| |||| ||||

I learned a lot through my 121 first dates. I developed ways to take care of and protect myself. I learned how to grow from my mistakes. I created rules to live by that served me. But sometimes you might need to throw all the rules, or at least caution, to the wind when you're so called. I met my partner, my match, the one I am supposed to be with for the second part of my life. The one who knows I'm a handful but has big enough hands to deal with me. The one who's so similar that we often joke about how we're the same person, except where the delicious polarity of our masculine and feminine energies comes into play.

If all my sorting filters had been turned on and functioning, Date #121 and I never would have met. I would have hit that X in the top right corner of his profile box and he would have disappeared from my search forever before we even said hello, and that would have been the biggest tragedy of all.

In November 2013 we had our commitment ceremony and moved in together. And we live happily ever after in San Francisco.

Acknowledgments

I never intended to have (or write about) 121 dates, but first date #54 was so horrendous that I had to share, and from that, my blog was created—mostly to convey to my married friends that the grass isn't always greener in the town of Singleville. I would like to thank Date #54 for his inspiration, Date #51 for further prompting me to be out with my experiences, and all my loyal blog readers who would diligently email me to ask, "When are you going on another date?" You kept me dating and you kept me writing. There wouldn't be a book without you.

My most heartfelt thank-you to Dave Pierce (Date #121) for finally showing up. You are definitely worth the wait, and I'd go on another 120 just to get to you.

Respect and appreciation to each and every one of the 120 men I dated—some of you for a minute, some of you for quite a while. Thank you for being willing to take yourself away from your life for an evening or three or a hundred to spend time with me.

My deepest love and adoration to Lilly-Bee and Eloise, my two ever-steady dog companions. You saved me when you let me cry into your neck, when you licked my face, loved me unconditionally, and gave me the snuggling-up that a single girl needs.

Extra-special thanks to all my dating allies. I never would have made it through to the other side of the dating process as a (mostly) kind person without you. Love and gratitude to Leslie Thomsen, Denise Lynn, Robert Corrington, Melissa Comito-Aakre, Michelle Keane, Regina Martinelli, Shadee Ardalan, Alisa Highfill, Sarah Jane Keskula, and the entire (and extended) Gerbode clan for being a loving and supportive family to me.

Much love to Susan Bailess for having the strength and good sense of humor to handle the fact that your daughter is a serious over-sharer.

Deep gratitude and love to Bob Newman, the best ex-husband ever. Thank you for proofreading my entire manuscript before I handed it over to the publisher. Thank you for staying in my life after the romantic part of our relationship was over. You are my family and I will always be here for you.

Respect and big love to Alison Armstrong. Thank you for changing the world and for teaching me to love, trust, and value men as a gender, not just the chosen two or three I kept in my back pocket before 2002. Thank you for giving me access to a world of men who want to protect, provide for, and make me happy.

To the thousands of men I've interviewed, I appreciate your invaluable contribution to my life, and to the thousands of women who've let me teach and coach you, thank you for allowing me to make that difference and for all I've learned from you.

I am eternally grateful to my book angel, Linda Sivertsen, who gave me notes on the book and who helped me connect with my agent. You have everything to do with the success of this book. CJ Schepers for helping with the hardest part of my book proposal. My literary agent, Laura Yorke, who took a chance on a girl without a large platform—thanks for seeing the potential in my words. I am profoundly grateful to Emily Han, acquisitions editor at Beyond Words, for saying, "Yes, let's do this." Landing this publishing deal felt like the luckiest day of my life. And to Sylvia Spratt, developmental editor, for making my words funny, clear, and not quite so damned absolute. Thanks to Lindsay Brown, managing editor, and Anna Noak, acquisitions editor, for making sure this book goes out into the world in a beautiful way; and to everyone at Beyond Words and Simon & Schuster for the contributions you made for this project to happen. To Sean Klein and Charlotte Huggins for giving me much-needed feedback. Thanks for helping me be a better writer.

Big thanks to Bernadette, Matthew, and John at Dirty Water SF for helping and supporting this project. Thanks to every café that let me overstay my welcome while I wrote and sipped free iced-tea refills. From Community Café in Sonoma, where I gained five pounds from a lack of willpower over their homemade desserts, to the Depot in Mill Valley, where the baristas all knew me and kindly pretended they didn't when I was on a coffee date, to Farley's East, the safest café in Oakland if you're trying to avoid a laptop robbery, to Wicked Grounds, my favorite café in San Francisco—right down to the random kitty person sauntering around on all fours before picking the red velvet chair to curl up in for a catnap. And finally, to John Coltrane, who gave me sound without distracting lyrics to override whatever was happening in cafés as I wrote this book.

Notes

Part I

2. Getting Ready for Your Dating Adventure

1. Sheila Kelley, "S Factor Fitness," homepage, accessed April 21, 2015, http://www.sfactor.com.
2. "Let's Get Naked: Sheila Kelley at TEDxAmericanRiviera," YouTube video, 21:06, posted by TEDx Talks, December 18, 2012, https://www.youtube.com/watch?v=Lrdn4lazVBc.

3. Dos and Don'ts Before the First Date

3. Barry R. Komisaruk, Carlos Beyer-Flores, and Beverly Whipple, *The Science of Orgasm* (Baltimore: Johns Hopkins University Press, 2006), 63.

7. Where Are All the Single Ones?

4. Stephanie Losee and Helaine Olen, *Office Mate: The Employee Handbook for Finding—and Managing—Romance on the Job* (New York: Adams Media, 2007), 55.
5. Ibid., 14.

8. Online Dating Sites: Where Your Dates Look When They're Looking for You

6. Sheena S. Iyengar and Mark R. Lepper, "When Choice is Demotivating: Can One Desire Too Much of a Good Thing?" *Journal of Personality and Social Psychology* 79, no. 6 (2000): 995–1006, http://werbepsychologie-uamr.de/files /literatur/01_Iyengar_Lepper(2000)_Choice-Overload.pdf.
7. Katherine Fritz, "Dating Is the Worst, and Other Scientific Facts," *Huffington Post*, September 2013, http://www.huffingtonpost.com/katherine-fritz/dating -is-the-worst-and-other-scientific-facts_b_3972843.html.

11. How to Find Your Mate Online

8. Louann Brizendine, *The Female Brain* (New York: Random House, 2007), 59.
9. Sheril Kirshenbaum, *The Science of Kissing: What Our Lips Are Telling Us* (New York: Grand Central Publishing, 2011), 109.

Part II

13. Converting Online to the Real World

1. Louann Brizendine, *The Female Brain* (New York: Random House, 2007), 63.
2. Barry R. Komisaruk, Carlos Beyer-Flores, and Beverly Whipple, *The Science of Orgasm* (Baltimore: Johns Hopkins University Press, 2006), 9.

15. On Your First Date

3. Alison Armstrong, "In Sync with the Opposite Sex: Understand the Conflicts. End the Confusion. Make The Right Choices." Directed by Alison Armstrong (Glendore, CA: PAX Programs, 2006), Audio CD, disc 3, track 12, 1:50.

17. Sorting Your Mate

4. Linda A. Jackson, *Physical Appearance and Gender: Sociobiological and Socio-cultural Perspectives*, SUNY Series, the Psychology of Women Series (New York: State University of New York Press, 1992), 172.